Reflections on the
Revolution in Europe

CHATTO
CounterBlasts

Ralf

DAHRENDORF

Reflections
on the Revolution
in Europe

*In a letter intended to have been sent to a
gentleman in Warsaw, 1990*

Chatto & Windus
LONDON

Published in 1990 by
Chatto & Windus Ltd
20 Vauxhall Bridge Road
London SW1V 2SA

A CIP catalogue record for this book
is available from the British Library

ISBN 0 7011 3725 8

Photoset in Linotron Ehrhardt by
Rowland Phototypesetting Ltd
Bury St Edmunds, Suffolk
Printed in Great Britain by
St Edmundsbury Press Ltd
Bury St Edmunds, Suffolk

Dear Mr J.,

When at the end of my recent trip to your country, I came to see you on that sunny morning in early March, I expected us to sit down to a cup of coffee and chat a little about current affairs in the manner of what the French sometimes call *café de commerce*. The winter was odd, was it not? Stormy, but mild. The 'greenhouse effect,' no doubt. In fact, it may have saved Gorbachev. At any rate, it reduced his energy bill . . . But you never allowed such small talk to begin. Instead you showered me with questions about the riddles of Poland and Europe after the revolution of 1989 until I was too dazed to answer any of them properly. Only now, in the quiet of my Oxford study, surrounded by books and papers and gazing out at the friendly motley of the buildings of St Antony's College, do I find the resources to try to respond to you properly.

What does it all mean, and where is it going to lead (you wanted to know)? Are we not witnessing a process of dissolution without anything taking the place of the old and admittedly dismal structures? How can political parties emerge (you asked for example) when the old ones of 1946 and of the interwar years have become irrelevant, and new parties are unable to find a social base to sustain them? And why (you added almost anxiously) had I written some time ago that not only socialism, but social democracy was on the way out? What is the market economy going to do to the social texture of the country? Will it not make some rich while the many get poorer than ever? What will happen to cultural life? Do we have to read and watch trash now that we are free and no longer have cheap books and subsidised quality films? How can we bring about the rule of law? Have not the old judges lost all credibility while we cannot find new ones which guarantee independence and objectivity? And what about the German menace? Are we not going to see a balkanised Europe dominated by the one power which is uniting rather than disintegrating? Was I (you inquired) on balance hopeful so far as the new Europe is concerned, or anxious and worried like many of your compatriots, and as you gathered, others in East Central Europe as well?

Hopes and fears depend, of course, on expectations. Your sense of apprehension may be caused by the very things which make me feel optimistic. Did I detect, somewhere behind all those questions, a vision of the future of your country and others in a similar position which is as understandable as it is unreal and therefore misleading? You seemed to envisage a society which is both contained by strict precepts of public and private morality, and economically vigorous and thriving, one that is both dominated by a sense of order and discipline, and politically pluralistic – a 'Sweden' perhaps. You will note the quotation marks. 'Sweden' is not Sweden; it is a dream with no base anywhere on the map of Europe. What is more, we must thank our lucky stars that there is no 'Sweden' in the real world, for if it existed, it would be located somewhere between Lee Kuan Yew's Singapore, which finds it difficult to accept even one opposition member in its 'parliament' and charges a penalty of two hundred dollars for dropping litter in the street, and Plato's Republic, in which philosopher-kings see to it that dissidence cannot arise because they alone are in possession of the truth. The real Sweden, fortunately, is a free country, with much (though perhaps not enough) of the untidiness and multifariousness, disorderliness and heterogeneity, conflict and changeability which allow the blossoming of human life chances, and of humans with them.

But your questions deserve more than a simple defence of Sweden against 'Sweden'. Moreover, it is not my intention to attack you for your views which deserve respect even if one does not share them. Above all, your questions deserve answers. As I began to put my two fingers to the typewriter, it soon became clear that my response would exceed the normal dimensions of a letter. I hope you will bear with me, nevertheless, though there is one inconvenience which must be dealt with. A letter allows a certain informality of style, digressions and overlaps and imbalances of many kinds which would be less acceptable in a treatise. But it is long, and so I have chosen a halfway house (despite the argument against a 'third way' which lies at the heart of my reply) and identified four major sections of this missive. None of them fits tidily under a simple heading, but it would be true to describe the first as being mostly about revolutions and the open society; the second mostly about the strange death of socialism and the mirage of a 'third way'; the third mostly about politics, economics and the road to freedom; and the fourth mostly about Germany and the new architecture of Europe.

Mostly about Revolutions and the Open Society

The person to whom you addressed your questions is one of those who will forever cherish the memory of the events of 1989. What a time to be alive! Yes, there were tears, bitter tears at the massacre of Tiananmen Square which brutally ended the 'democracy movement' of students and workers and even soldiers in China, tears for the victims of *securitate* brutality in Timisoara and elsewhere in Romania six months later. But most of the tears in 1989 were tears of joy. Who can ever forget the moment when your first non-communist Prime Minister, Tadeusz Mazowiecki, took his seat on the government benches in the Sejm on 24 August, looking slightly forlorn with his sad and pensive expression, but quite obviously not a dictator or a *nomenklatura* bureaucrat? What could erase from memory the jubilation at the breaching of the Berlin Wall on 9 November, with those who had been separated for twenty-eight years embracing each other and their erstwhile guards joining in the celebrations? Who could hold back emotions when

4

Vaclav Havel emerged, in what was probably his only two-piece suit and tie, as the new President of Czechoslovakia on 29 December? And talking about images (for it was a year of television too), anyone who watched the slipping countenance of the Romanian dictator Nicolae Ceauçescu during the mass meeting organised by his agents on 21 December, which turned into an angry demonstration against him as he was speaking, will forever know what it means that the rulers lose their nerve before the people get their way.

There is no need for me to remind you of the sequence of events in that *annus mirabilis*, 1989. In any case, their memorable history has now found a chronicler, Timothy Garton Ash, who combines passion and insight like few other instant historians before him. (I have benefited from his advice in setting out to answer your questions.) In his book *We the People*, he keeps alive 'the revolution of '89' as he witnessed it in Warsaw, Budapest, Berlin and Prague. Was it really a revolution? The question may seem academic, of more interest to university students than to those involved. Garton Ash himself has coined the term *refolution* for the events of Warsaw and Budapest, because they were in essence *ref*orms from above in response to the pressure for rev*olution* from below, though he uses *revolution* freely for what happened in Prague, Berlin and Bucharest. Clearly, the changes brought about by the events of 1989 were both extremely rapid and very radical (which is one definition of revolutions). At the end of the day, they led to the delegitimation of an entire ruling class and the replacement of most of its key members, as well as a constitutional transformation with far-reaching consequences.

Most of the time it does not matter what name we give to historical events. But for once the academic is of considerable practical significance. Crane Brinton has taught us, by comparing the events of England in 1688, America in 1776, France in 1789 and Russia in 1917 that revolutions have their own 'anatomy'. Not only their causes can be traced but also their course. They all begin with a honeymoon after the victory over the old regime is achieved without serious bloodshed, as 'the way is open to the regeneration men have been so long talking about, so long hoping for'. Brinton quotes Wordsworth:

France standing on the top of golden hours,
And human nature seeming born again.

Not all have shared this sentiment, notably not the author of whom more will have to be said in this letter, Edmund Burke. But in the countries concerned, the honeymoon was a time of rejoicing. It was also short. Some of Brinton's statements sound ominous today: 'In the first stages, and at the critical moment when the test of force comes, the old regime is faced by solid opposition. [But] the opposition is indeed composed of various groups, is never quite that over-simplification, a "united people".' This soon becomes evident as the 'rule of the moderates' commences. The old opposition falls apart; it never really manages to combine the task of building a new constitution with that of governing; some radicals begin to claim that the moderates have betrayed the revolution and are not going far enough. As the moderates fail to get a grip on things, the extremists sense their hour. They are a minority, but they are organised and fighting fit. Finally, they overthrow the ineffectual moderates, and the 'reigns of terror and virtue' begin. They are terrible. By the time the Thermidor sets an end to them – as the fall of Robespierre in July 1794, which led to more 'normal' though hardly much more agreeable conditions, to Napoleon, or after the death of Lenin in Soviet Russia, to Stalin – societies have reached the limits of their endurance. Dictators take over a scene of decline, destruction and demoralisation.

Many have doubted whether Crane Brinton's gloomy analysis applies even to 'his' revolutions, and notably to the 'glorious revolution' in England and the revolutionary acts which created the United States of America. Edmund Burke argues eloquently that the whole point of 1688 was to prevent a revolution like that in France in 1789, and George Washington was hardly a Napoleon, let alone a Stalin. Some parallels of anatomy are nevertheless unmistakable in 1989 and 1990. For a while, if sometimes a short while, opposition groups like Solidarity in Poland, the Civic Forum in Czechoslovakia, even Ecoglasnost in Bulgaria and the early Committee for National Salvation in Romania were united. They wanted to replace an old regime, and they did so. But the honeymoon did not last. It could not last. Once the common enemy had disappeared, more normal divisions within the hitherto united opposition emerged, like industrial and rural Solidarity, and other groups of Christian-democratic and nationalist persuasion, or the political parties which took the place of the Civic Forum in Czechoslovakia and the New Forum in East Germany. Also, the sudden rise to power changes the complexion of things. Government requires different talents from opposition, and even different virtues, a practical 'ethics of responsibility' instead of the pure 'ethics of conviction'. To make matters worse, the removal of the old regime leaves a vacuum. Unlike the winners of a democratic election, revolutionary leaders have to start from scratch. Seeking legitimacy by elections, and accepting certain checks and balances is all very well, but with the demise of the monopoly of the party, the whole structure of government has collapsed. Who removes and appoints officials at all levels, and how are the new people found? How are taxes levied? How is a new policy of ownership implemented? How do new curricula reach every school in the country? You raised the question of what takes the place of the dismantled structures of yesterday, and the answer is that to begin with, there is little more than enthusiasm and hope.

Brinton is a trifle unkind to the moderates who take over during the revolutionary honeymoon. Their failure, he argues, is not so much a tragedy as their own fault; they do not have the courage of their convictions: 'They used grand words and phrases grandly as a consolation and joy to their listeners and to themselves. But they did not believe in them as the radicals believed in them; they did not intend to try to pursue them to their logical conclusions in action.' Somehow this does not ring true with respect to President Havel, or your own Prime Minister and his finance minister Leszek Balcerowicz. Yet the collapse of the centre is characteristic of several post-communist countries in Europe. They have shed the monopolistic party, the security police, the claims of the *nomenklatura* and of course the ever-present threat of Soviet intervention, but with few exceptions they have not been able to put much more than good intentions in their place. As a result, old regional, ethnic, religious rivalries reappear, and new cleavages threaten to disrupt the unity of purpose which brought about change.

Democracy, in the sense of asking the people to decide, will not fill this vacuum. 'We the people' can rise against an abhorrent regime of exploitation and suppression, but 'we the people' cannot govern. The democratic illusion that there is such a thing as government by the people has always been an invitation to usurpers and new monopolies. Beware of the errors of an earlier generation, which included men like Robert Michels! He was one of those who believed that socialism would change everything, including the government of the many by the few. Then he discovered that socialist parties were just as likely to generate ruling minorities as all other parties. In his dismay, he formulated (in 1911, borrowing heavily from an earlier work by Ostrogorski) the 'iron law of oligarchy': 'Whoever says organisation, states a tendency towards oligarchy.' As a result, Michels first despaired of socialist parties, then of human nature, and finally fell for the fascist cult of the leader, albeit of the Mussolini variety, as a way out. There is truth in the 'iron law' but no reason for despair. The important point is to check and balance ruling groups, and to replace them from time to time by peaceful means, such as elections. More than that, these groups are needed. Democracy is a form of government, not a steam bath of popular feelings. It needs those who lead as much as those who put a halt to apparent errors of policy and to the arrogance of power.

It was clear that the euphoria of 1989 would give way to a more sober mood in 1990. Breaching and breaking up the wall, and selling its pieces for hard currency, is a wonderful and even lucrative experience, but building a new city takes time and a heavy toll of emotions, energies and resources. Also, as history slows down, there are risks. Driving a car on an icy road is all right as long as the road is dead straight and one does not change gear. One can drive quite fast in fact, and the revolution of 1989 recognised no speed limits at all. Now, however, we encounter bends and tricky traffic conditions, and we have to change gear. It requires unusual skill not to swerve and crash into others or be thrown off the road altogether.

But let me contain such doubts for a little while yet

and note the assets which 1989 has created. One of them in particular deserves notice, because without it I could not even have started this letter to you. It has been called the reunification of language. I heard André Fontaine, the thoughtful editor of *Le Monde*, speak about the three unifications which we are experiencing: the reunification of Germany which, as I know, is for you more a headache than a source of delight; the reunification of Europe which is central to my replies to your questions; and 'a reunification in our language'. Fontaine reminds us of 'the hollow rhetoric of the past', the many dialogues of the deaf, the exchange of platitudes in political negotiations, scholarly conferences and even personal encounters. He could have spoken also of the absurd balance sheets drawn up between systems: You have no censorship, but we have no unemployment. Social rights compensate for the absence of political rights. – All this cant is suddenly swept away like a bad dream by the light of day. Fontaine tells of an East-West seminar with dissidents, émigrés and some who had stayed in their academies and institutes, 'and they all used the same words and concepts and spoke of the same things'.

The reunification of language encapsulates the story which needs to be told. Two systems based on two ways of looking at the world needed two languages. How did George Orwell introduce Newspeak? 'The purpose of Newspeak,' he wrote in *Nineteen Eighty-four*, 'was not only to provide a medium of expression for the world-view and mental habits proper to the devotees of [the ruling ideology] Ingsoc, but to make all other modes of thought impossible.' By accepting that the other side uses its own concepts and phrases, the two systems were stabilised. As long as the two languages held, nothing would change. We had got used to the fact that even valued notions like democracy or human rights had different meanings on the two sides of the Iron Curtain. One tried to read between the lines, listened to the slightest nuance to detect signs of change, went for walks on the beach or even in the woods, but usually the most that would emerge was a stilted joint declaration. Distance had to be emphasised. People read my books, but they never commented on them without calling me a 'bourgeois author', and many on this side of the fence found it necessary to apply analogous epithets to authors from the other side. Suddenly, all this is gone. We meet, and we talk as we would anywhere. We may need interpreters, but we do not need what Orwell called 'ideological translation'. This means that language no longer serves to stabilise two systems. Conversation, discussion can actually change views. We have entered an era of change. A dreadful wall has crumbled and is in the process of being removed altogether.

How did this happen? Why did the revolution occur? And why did it occur in 1989? Many reasons can be given, some proximate, some remote. 'It took a generation which did not know that it could not be done,' said one of your countrymen with a neat paradox. Older people had been discouraged by the experiences of 1956 and 1968 and other, smaller revolts;

the young had a go because they did not realise that it was impossible to dislodge regimes, and so they dislodged them. Each country in East Central Europe has its own history and political culture. One of the delights of 1989 is the rediscovery of these differences. Thus every country deserves its own explanation. Yet when all is said and done, three points can be made for all communist countries in Europe.

The first has a name, Mikhail Gorbachev. You may wonder why I have not mentioned him since the first paragraph of this letter. One reason is that the European house which you and I want to turn into our common home ends where the Soviet Union, or whatever succeeds it, begins. This is a consequential statement, and the case for it has to be made. But I do not mean to detract from Gorbachev's role in the events of 1989. They would not have happened then and in the particular way in which they occurred had it not been for the President of the Soviet Union and his remarkable approach. So far as East Central Europe is concerned, it is best summed up in the words of Gorbachev's foreign-ministry spokesman, the ever-alert Gennady Gerasimov. On 25 October 1989, when asked whether the Soviet Union still adhered to the Brezhnev Doctrine, which threatened recalcitrant allies with military intervention, Gerasimov replied by introducing (on the spur of the moment?) the Sinatra Doctrine: 'Sinatra had a song, "I did it my way . . ." So every country decides in its own way which road to take.' Sinatra's song was actually a sad little piece about an old man's 'final curtain' when 'the end is near', but never mind. They do 'it' their way. Two aspects of 'it' are relevant. One is that the Soviet army will no longer intervene when its allies go their own way; the other is that the Soviet Party will not insist on the monopoly of the Communist Party in these countries. In fact, this means the release of the satellites into independence (though sadly, it is not applied in the same way to the Baltic republics or the other parts of the Soviet Union).

What made Gorbachev take this line? What indeed makes him tick? Professor Archie Brown, a man who has followed Gorbachev's career from its earliest stages, and who predicted his unique significance before he even became General Secretary, has examined various theories. It is true, he says, that Gorbachev has learned very quickly on the job; it is also true that he has increased his power systematically, even as he was in part undoubtedly swept along by events. The critical fact, however, is his frame of mind: 'One of Gorbachev's most important characteristics is a relatively open mind . . . Gorbachev is the most pragmatic leader in Soviet history, but that does not mean that he is an unprincipled one. The Soviet Union today – with all its problems – is a far more open society than the country whose leadership he inherited. And that at least was the way he intended it to develop.' It would not be too far-fetched to say that Gorbachev is above all an opener of hitherto closed doors. He hopes that those who walk through them will end up where he wants them to go, probably with some kind of 'democratic socialism', but in the first instance he wants to unlock the door into an open future.

The Sinatra Doctrine does precisely that. It reminds me of the liberal doctrine of Frederick the Great of Prussia in the eighteenth century: *Ein jeder soll nach seiner Facon selig werden*: let everyone find his blessings in his own way. Some chose the Catholic, others the Protestant, the Jewish or even the agnostic way. In East Central Europe, the first step was to abandon the monopoly of the Communist Party and encourage political alternatives. This in fact was the revolution of 1989, from which many other developments follow.

Why would there be such strong pressure to remove the state party from its monopoly position? Because – and this is the second unifying point – communism never worked. In East Central Europe at least it was an imposed regime of suppression which from the beginning gave rise to resistance and violent conflict. The uprisings of 1953 in East Germany, 1956 in Hungary, 1968 in Czechoslovakia, 1980 in Poland were not just episodes; they were all protests endemic to what has now become the old regime. This, moreover, is not a discovery after the event. Few have foreseen the dramatic sequence of changes in 1989, but many have expected them to happen at some point. In my book *Class and Class Conflict in Industrial Society*, I wrote in 1959 that 'a tendency towards violent conflict and sudden change accompanies totalitarian countries in every phase of their development'. Conflict can be suppressed. Such suppression may even

15

be fairly effective if certain safety valves are created (I referred to the frequency of 'meetings' and 'discussions' and the mechanisms of mobilisation in communist countries as examples). But in the end it will fail. 'Suppression defeats its own ends: totalitarian governments are in "danger" of being violently overthrown to the extent to which they resort to suppression as a means of dealing with conflict.'

This explains Ceauçescu's Romania, though not necessarily the other countries of East Central Europe. After spending a year in the Soviet Union, Ernest Gellner has recently pointed out a peculiar dilemma for the ideology of Gorbachev's *perestroika*. Insofar as any ideology is still effective, the official line is to hold on to the October Revolution and Lenin's heritage as the 'legitimate orthodoxy'. However, the early years of the Soviet Union were followed not by one, but by two 'usurpations and perversions'. 'The first of these,' notes Gellner, 'was of course Stalinism and the cult of personality, with its total arbitrariness. The second was the period of stagnation, marked by bureaucratic rigidity, corruption, cynicism, and still devoid of democracy and the rule of law, even if not so massively guilty of Stalinist excesses.' Stalinism and Brezhnevism are, in other words, different. The former may well be called totalitarian; it is geared to one leader and his whims, and embarks on a permanent revolution, on terror and a path to catastrophe. The other, however, is authoritarian. Its hallmark is a *nomenklatura* whose vested interest leads it to exploit the rest of the people at the risk of stagnation and decline. Suppression serves to cement the power of this fairly large ruling group which, with its families and retainers, may well have comprised close to 10 per cent of the population in communist countries. But contrary to totalitarianism, such authoritarian rule does not require a regime of terror nor even permanent mobilisation. If people shut up and withdraw to their niches of privacy while doing what they are required to do, they will be pushed about and sometimes harassed, but they will not be persecuted with the systematic arbitrariness of total rule.

Total rule breeds violence, but stagnation in the end leads to uncontrollably rapid and radical change as well. When I wrote *The New Liberty* in 1975, I argued that revolts and uprisings 'are endemic to societies in which those at the bottom of social hierarchies including labour are no better off than anywhere else, the place of capital is taken by a new class of political bureaucrats, and that of wage disputes and strikes, or elections and changes of government by complex procedures of unwilling adaptation which are always liable to break down.' Without safety valves (I argued at the time), latent conflicts are bound to become manifest especially if expansion, economic growth, stops. Thirteen years later, only months before the beginning of the revolution in 1989, I wrote again, in *The Modern Social Conflict*, that the 'leaden mixture of autocracy and bureaucracy' which we call 'really existing socialism' cannot last. 'For the majority, really existing socialism is a pretty pure form of what it pretends to have overcome, exploitation, except that the regime is sufficiently incompetent in economic matters to make sure that there is not a great deal to exploit.' One book I unfortunately did not write, though I had thought of it as early as the mid-1970s. It was supposed to be called *Nineteen Eighty-nine*, and it would have shown that even Orwell's world of *Nineteen Eighty-four* could not last. I wish I had written it, though extricating Winston Smith from the fangs of Big Brother would have been even more difficult than it was to extricate the Romanian intellectuals from Ceauçescu's *securitate*.

This leads to the third line of explanation for the events of 1989. Gorbachev opened the door; suppressed conflicts were bound to explode; and the strange history of the 1980s provided the slow-match to the powderkeg. An Italian journalist recently asked me, 'Why is it that the most anti-social decade in recent history made the West so attractive for the East?' There is a lot wrong with this question, but it is true that the rich countries of the world have passed through a decade of spectacular economic growth without much regard for those who were disadvantaged or too weak to come on board. The majority has done rather well in these years, more so in some countries than in others, but to a notable extent everywhere in Western Europe, North America and Japan.

One aspect of this revival is as important from your point of view as it is from ours. Europe has found its self-confidence again. Not so long ago, everyone talked about 'Eurogloom', 'Europessimism' and

'Eurosclerosis'. People were prepared to write the old continent off. But somehow, almost miraculously – or was it the work of the President of the European Commission, Jacques Delors, and the Single European Act? – the idea and reality of Europe began to take off again. The European Community defined a new objective for itself, the achievement of a Single Market by the end of 1992 which embodies the 'four freedoms' of the movement of goods, services, capital and people. With this new objective, the mood changed, and people began to talk about more distant horizons, economic and monetary union, closer co-operation in the fields of foreign policy and defence.

All this was in part a response to our own Western version of Brezhnevism, the stagnation, or worse, stagflation of the 1970s. Mancur Olson, who wrote about it in *The Rise and Decline of Nations*, believed that only war or revolution could get us out of the rut; in the event, neoliberal governments of the right and the left did the trick, insofar as governments can ever be held responsible for economic change. The 1980s saw the rebirth of the entrepreneur, with all his creative and destructive qualities.

The price of this new economic miracle was high, and since you may yet have to pay it along with those of us who live in the more fortunate parts of Europe, it is worth mentioning. A part of the price is indeed social. In most Western countries, an underclass of long-term unemployed or persistently poor people has emerged – a living indictment of our values if not a threat to the fabric of our societies. The deeper cost, however, may yet turn out to be partly economic and partly moral. The '80s were in Susan Strange's phrase, a decade of 'casino capitalism'. Money was generated by money rather than by the creation of lasting wealth. The movements of shares on the major stock exchanges, for example, bore little relation to real growth, and the crashes of 1987 and 1989 were largely capricious. Moreover, private and public debt fuelled much of the growth. In the United States, the result has already become a major issue of public concern. None of this has added to the moral integrity and strength of Western societies. Greed, fraud and short-term thinking have all too frequently replaced thrift, honest business and a longer perspective, to say nothing of concern for others.

Thus the West is by no means as rosy as you tended to paint it when we talked. But it now emerges that the decade of new growth in our world was one of continued stagnation if not decline in yours. Available figures on economic conditions are almost worthless. We now know that there was, and still is, no proper national accounting in the communist countries. Also, international statistical agencies have been far too credulous in accepting government-fabricated information. The German Democratic Republic was certainly nowhere near as advanced as we were led to believe. The relationship of its gross domestic product per capita to that of the Federal Republic of Germany was not, as some statistics suggested, 1:2, but more like 1:5, indeed 1:7. However, even official figures for the six countries of East Central Europe show a pretty dismal picture for the years 1980–88, with slow export growth and much slower growth of imports, high indebtedness in many cases, and modest per capita GDP, to say nothing of real wages.

What we did not know before we reunified language (though we might have known had we listened to some of the independent voices 'from underneath') was the extent of the physical, social and moral degradation of the countries of communist Europe. It looks as if an increasingly anxious *nomenklatura* had squeezed every penny out of their countries without investing in the future or even caring about people's elementary needs. The housing stock was allowed to deteriorate badly. Public services now require vast sums for repair if not reconstruction. The much-vaunted social services turn out to be primitive and ineffectual. And all this was accompanied by what George Kennan calls a 'culture of pretence'. While no one believed the state ideology any more, it was taught in the schools and millions were exposed to the acid rain of an ageing Newspeak day after dismal day. Surely, as Kennan observes, 'when a given regime is no longer able to carry on without accommodating itself to a wide-ranging pretence that it shares with its subject people, the artificiality of that pretence being perfectly evident to both sides, then its ultimate fall must be considered as inevitable and probably imminent, even if no one can tell when and how it will occur.'

In the 1950s and 1960s, the countries of the West grew fast and far, and those of the East much more slowly; but both went in the same direction. In the

1980s, they moved in opposing directions until the contrast became untenable. The more demoralised East Europeans became, the more attractive seemed the new-found confidence of Western Europe. The more the conditions of public and private life deteriorated in the East, the more they improved in the West, and people knew it. One does not need to be a Marxian to predict trouble in such a predicament. Whoever watched Western television knew that the productive forces for a better life existed, indeed they existed right next door; it was thus about time to transform the communist mode of production and the entire superstructure built upon it. The revolution could not be far off. It happened in 1989.

What did it do? You did not ask me this question. Perhaps you assumed that we both knew the answer. After all, it made us speak a common language. But there must be more to this revolution for hundreds of thousands to take to the streets. It certainly changed the way in which we perceive the world, and probably its real balance of power in the process. For decades, we have spoken of the First, the Second and the Third Worlds. We have assumed that the First and the Second are competing for the Third World, or at least for its votes in the United Nations, since neither capitalists nor communists have done a great deal for those who were left behind by economic development. The very concept of a Third World presupposes two others. One of these has now all but disappeared from the scene. There is only one world left with serious claims to development and hegemony (as Fidel Castro and one or two other relics of the past have discovered to their dismay). The First and the Second Worlds are being reunited into something which has no name yet, nor a number; perhaps it will just be the World.

With this process, an intricate if somewhat dubious equilibrium has been upset. There was the European Community (or perhaps, the twenty-three-member OECD – Organisation for Economic Co-operation and Development) on one side, and Comecon on the other. NATO was balanced by the Warsaw Pact, the Federal Republic of Germany by the German Democratic Republic. All this is no longer, or at any rate, it has lost its force. An old system of co-ordinates needs to be adjusted. Such changes are undoubtedly important. Yet they do not answer the question of what the revolution in Europe has achieved beyond the dismantling of yesterday's structures. When some of us discussed this issue, the French historian François Furet remarked: 'With all the fuss and noise, not a single new idea has come out of Eastern Europe in 1989.' Furet has deflated in his scholarship the more hyperbolic interpretations of the French Revolution; it is therefore perhaps not surprising that he should try to do the same with that of Europe. But he has a point. In its core, the European revolution of 1989 is the rejection of an unbearable and, as we have seen, untenable reality, and by the same token it is a reaffirmation of old ideas. Democracy has hardly been invented in East Central Europe in 1989, nor has pluralism. Timothy Garton Ash points out that somehow communism 'did not manage to poison the words "citizen" and "civic"'; and that citizenship and civil society are therefore guiding lights of the new march to freedom; yet these too are not exactly new ideas.

Do we need new ideas to make a revolution real? In any case, how new were the ideas of the French or American revolutions? They were not pristine, to be sure; one can always trace ideas back into history. But the two revolutions set in motion the creative modern conflict between those who seek more entitlements and those who want more provisions, advocates of citizenship and advocates of growth, who between them (and sometimes together) serve to enhance the life chances of all. The revolution in Europe is not about a new idea in this sense. On the contrary; Garton Ash has put it well: 'The ideas whose time has come are old, familiar, well-tested ones. (It is the new ideas whose time has passed.)' And of all the well-tested ideas the most important is the fundamental discovery of modernity, the open society. Humans are fallible, and the human condition is uncertain. No one knows all the answers; at any rate no one can tell whether the answers on offer are right or wrong. Therefore we have to try to find the truth but make sure that if we err, or are thought to err, it is possible to try again. There is no greater danger to human liberty than dogma, the monopoly of one group, one ideology, one system. By the same token, the greatest task is to keep our affairs open for change. The open society does not promise an easy life. Indeed, human beings have a dangerous penchant for the cosiness of

24

a closed world. But if we want to move forward and improve ourselves and the conditions in which men and women live on this planet, we have got to accept the untidy, antagonistic, uncomfortable, but proud and encouraging prospect of open horizons. 'We can return to the beasts,' Karl Popper has said, 'but if we wish to remain human, then there is only one way, the way into the open society.'

Popper wrote *The Open Society and Its Enemies* during the Second World War; it was first published in 1945. His fellow Austrian emigrant to Britain, Friedrich von Hayek, wrote and published *The Road to Serfdom* at much the same time. I recommend these books to you, if only because the events of 1989 mark the end of a story which began in the turmoil of hope and despair after 1945, when some grasped the chance of openness and others succumbed to serfdom. Both authors are still alive to see the fruits of their work. They have known each other since their early days; both are (perhaps somewhat surprisingly for those who do not know the great place well) former teachers at the London School of Economics. (Indeed, Hayek was instrumental in liberating Popper from his New Zealand exile and bringing him to LSE on the strength of the manuscript of *The Open Society*.) Though they seem siblings, however, they are in fact very different. Hayek has a fatal tendency to hold another system against that of socialism. It is a passive system to be sure, but one complete in itself and intolerant of untidy realities; I will come back to it presently because so many of your compatriots, not a few Czechs and even more Hungarians are taken in by Hayek. Popper on the contrary is a radical defender of liberty, of change without bloodshed, of trial and error, and also of an active march into the unknown, and thus of people who try to design their destiny. This epistle is a homily to Popper rather than to Hayek.

Who else can help in the present predicament of Europe? To whom do we turn for enlightenment? Many have compared the events of 1989 with those of 1848, when a great surge of liberal democratic sentiment swept the countries of Europe, parliaments were created, old assumptions challenged and new horizons explored. Alas! the episode remained brief and was followed by decades of reaction. Two great authors associated with the time are of course Alexis de Tocqueville and Karl Marx. No analyst of social and political events can ignore them. Yet they are strangely unhelpful today. Perhaps this is because neither of them really lived in their own present. De Tocqueville was trying to come to terms with the revolution which had dislodged his class in 1789, and Marx was forever dreaming of the future revolution which would put everything right. When it comes to action, de Tocqueville has little more to teach than a kind of heroic realism which accepts the inevitable with grace, and Marx's teaching has come to grief in 1989, if not long before.

I think we are better advised to go back to the 1780s, to the lessons of the great transformations of that time. As a manual of liberal democracy, *The Federalist Papers* are unsurpassed. There is also much to learn from the practical example of America's independence in freedom and the design of a constitution which has lasted for over two hundred years. Alexander Hamilton has more useful advice to give on the rule of law, and James Madison on civil society (as well as many other subjects) than most if not all contemporary authors.

Then there is Edmund Burke, who in 1790 wrote his *Reflections on the Revolution in France*, in the form of 'a letter intended to have been sent to a gentleman in Paris'. He was just over sixty years old at the time, and had a distinguished if at times controversial public career behind him. The French Revolution was barely one year old, and the rule of the moderates still almost intact. He could not know of the reign of terror, the Thermidor and Napoleon's ascendancy, which were to follow within the next five years. Despite some superficial analogies, Burke may at first sight seem an unlikely godfather of this letter. His is a great polemic against the destruction of the age of chivalry; this is an ode to the open society. Burke wrote out of dismay and disgust at the events in France; I am writing from a sense of delight and of hope in view of the events in Europe. Yet I share the underlying beliefs of the great Whig who, years earlier, had supported the American Revolution in his influential parliamentary speeches and his *Letter to the Sheriffs of Bristol on the Affairs of America*. Burke was an advocate of civil society ('If civil society be made for the advantage of man, all the advantages for which it is made become his right'); he accepted the untidiness of reality ('The nature of man is intricate; the objects of society are of the greatest possible complexity: and therefore no simple disposition or direction of power can be suitable either to man's nature, or to the quality of his affairs'); he abhorred the purveyors of systems, of total transformations ('It is with them a war or a revolution, or it is nothing'); and he defended the nearest approximation to an open society at the time, the English constitution.

The difference between Burke's letter to the gentleman in Paris and my letter to you is as much one of the nature of the events at issue as of the political temperament of the author. Burke did not want the constitution of England destroyed by an import of Utopian dogma. He minded the absolute, indeed total character of what he saw in Paris. I delight at the signs of an openness all over Europe which, far from being a threat to the British, the French, the German constitutions of liberty, reaffirm their principles and call upon us more fortunate Europeans to try to help – to help understand what is happening, and even to help lay foundations for the open society.

Hayek's *The Road to Serfdom* was a surprisingly gloomy book, considering the promises of a world which was about to quash the scourge of Nazism. Hayek did not see things this way. He thought that Britain was in danger of adopting the ideology of the defeated enemy. For two centuries ideas had moved from Britain eastwards (he said), but now the easterly winds of socialism prevailed in the world of ideas, and 'socialism means slavery'. 'The rise of Fascism and

Nazism,' Hayek warned, 'was not a reaction against the socialist trends of the preceding period, but a necessary outcome of those tendencies.' These trends had been imported into Britain from Germany, indeed there were now 'totalitarians in our midst'. Hayek went far in pursuing this thesis; to him, the British Labour Party seemed about to betray two centuries of liberal and capitalist beliefs, and create a proto-fascist state of collectivism and central planning in Britain. He not only attacked Harold Laski, his professorial colleague at the LSE, but said, 'We should never forget that the anti-semitism of Hitler has driven from his country, or turned into his enemies, many people who in every respect are confirmed totalitarians of the German type.'

Socialism, including democratic socialism, has remained Hayek's *bête noire* throughout his long life. More than forty years after *The Road to Serfdom*, he published another diatribe, *The Fatal Conceit*. In it he argued that socialism kills. 'The dispute between the market order and socialism is no less than a matter of survival. To follow socialist morality would destroy much of present humankind and impoverish much of the rest.' What is the alternative? The 'fatal conceit', for Hayek, lies in the belief 'that man is able to shape the world around him according to his wishes'. Hayek's alternative, capitalism, or the market order, has a curiously passive air about it. Its key is the renunciation of the belief in *Machbarkeit*, in the 'make-ability' of the world: 'For in fact we are able to bring about an ordering of the unknown *only by causing it to order itself.*' The italics are Hayek's; he obviously wanted to emphasise the point. There are 'natural, spontaneous, and self-ordering processes', and our only task, in the interest of liberty, is to establish rules of the game which allow them to hold their sway. Any attempt to speed them up or slow them down, to deflect or redirect them, is wrong, a sign of conceit, socialism.

Thus the scene is set for the great battle of systems, the 'natural' system of capitalism and the market order, and the 'conceited' system of socialism and planning. The point is important, if only because there are many, in your country and elsewhere in East Central Europe, who look to Hayek as the alternative which they can embrace now that Marx is dead. There is much to commend the economist and political theorist who has spent a lifetime campaigning for the constitution of liberty, but there is also a risk. Like Marx, Hayek knows all the answers. He does not find it easy to bear the untidiness of the real world. He gets as angry with those who have set out in his direction without following it through to the bitter end as he does with his ideological opponents. Hayek is an all-or-nothing theorist, which is fine so far as the constitutional preconditions of politics are concerned, but dangerous if not disastrous in the world of real political conflicts.

The distinction matters. Constitutional politics is about the framework of the social order, the social contract, as it were, and its institutional forms; normal politics is about the directions dictated by interests and other preferences within this framework. Having free and fair elections is a matter of constitutional politics, campaigning for the privatisation of the steel industry is a matter of normal politics. The distinction is not always clear. Some think, for example, that details like a 5 per cent threshold or regional party lists belong in the constitutional domain; I do not, but this merely goes to show that the boundary itself is a subject of dispute. Certainly Hayek is right when he argues that certain measures which appear to belong in the realm of economic ('normal') policy in fact have a constitutional dimension. This is clearly the case with the total nationalisation of private property. Indeed, in the 1970s many in Britain argued that liberty is at risk once government accounts for more than 60 per cent of GDP – though the figure is obviously arbitrary and the thesis is debatable.

In matters of constitutional politics there are no two ways, or rather there are only two ways, the closed and the open society, whereas in normal politics a hundred options may be on offer, and three or four usually are. Actually, the two concepts afford another way of describing what is happening in East Central Europe today. The revolution of 1989 was, like all revolutions, a period of constitutional politics. 'Democracy' and 'citizenship' are about the basic compact of liberty and in that sense beyond dispute, or else the subject of absolute and potentially violent conflicts. Revolutionary periods are abnormal times, in which normal politics is suspended. But gradually we see normal politics return, to the dismay of the constitutionalists perhaps, but arguably to the benefit of the majority. (I cannot conceal from you that my own interest is in constitutional politics above all, as you will not fail to notice in the course of this letter; but I realise of course that constitutions are merely the preconditions of what the political game is actually about. People do not really want to fight for the right to speak freely and to vote, or to choose their jobs and the goods they buy, they want to use these rights and speak or choose as they see fit.) Normal politics is messier than constitutional politics, but it is also closer to everyday life and thus to most people.

All this is relevant to Hayek (and to much else in my argument). I cannot fault Hayek on his constitutional politics, and would not try to do so, but he has an unfortunate tendency to turn all politics, and certainly most economic policy, constitutional. Like Hayek, I am intolerant of those who attack the foundations of liberty, but contrary to him I find it easy to tolerate those who advocate a major role for the state in economic policy-making, or a massive transfer of resources for social objectives, although I may be opposed to their views. Not everything that is disagreeable to some, or to me, or even to Hayek, has by the same token constitutional status. Whatever is raised to that plane is thereby removed from the day-to-day struggles of normal politics, until in the end a total constitution emerges in which there is nothing left to disagree about, a total society, another totalitarianism. One key to the future of the democratising societies of Europe is therefore the answer to the question of how and where the line is drawn between rules and principles which must be binding on all, and differences of view which can be fought out within these rules.

It is perhaps not surprising that Hayek's near-total constitutionalism made him view the course of events in the world with unrelenting gloom as late as 1988, when *The Fatal Conceit* was first published. After all, it is said that he regards even Margaret Thatcher as a traitor to the pure doctrine of Hayekism. Others who share Hayek's frame of mind, though hardly his erudition and perseverance, have interpreted the events of 1989 more airily and instantaneously as the triumph of capitalism over socialism. Let me spend a few moments on the State Department official Francis Fukuyama, who had his fifteen minutes of fame when he published a rather crude article entitled 'The End of History?' in the summer of 1989. The 'apocalyptic charge' of this article has even led an author in *Moscow News* to discuss it with perhaps undeserved politeness and caution.

Fukuyama says that he likes Hegel. History for him has a capital H; 'it' moves inexorably along paths only known to the world spirit, and whether we want it to move that way or not. (Hayek, we notice, is Hegel without History, or more plausibly perhaps, Fukuyama is Hayek set in historical motion.) History has done strange things in the twentieth century. It began in a liberal vein, but then created the socialist challenge. Indeed for a while it appeared as if the two were equivalent modes of social development; there was talk of convergence. At the end of the century, however, we see the 'unabashed victory of economic and political liberalism'. Moreover, 'the triumph of the West, of the Western *idea*' marks 'the end of history as such' because there are no fundamental conflicts of concepts of order left. Instead we begin to see the outline of what Fukuyama insists on calling a 'universal homogenous [*sic*!] state' which consists of 'liberal democracy in the political sphere combined with easy access to VCRs and stereos in the economic'. (VCRs and stereos indeed! I shudder to think of your reaction as I remember your concern about the destruction of culture by the consumer society.) Not all societies have reached this point, to be sure; many are still mired in history and will be for some time to come. In a subsequent article, Fukuyama also insisted that he had been misunderstood by those who read him as saying that nothing would happen any more; there were plenty of struggles ahead. But essentially the game is up. The triumph of one idea is not just a time for joy. 'The end of history will be a very sad time. The struggle for recognition, the willingness to risk one's life for a purely abstract goal, the worldwide, ideological struggle that called forth daring, courage, imagination, and idealism, will be replaced by economic calculation, the endless solving of technical problems, environmental concerns, and the satisfaction of sophisticated consumer demands.' VCRs and stereos again, no doubt. But who knows? 'Perhaps this very prospect of centuries of boredom at the end of history will serve to get history started once again.'

Caricatures make their point by exaggerating the characteristic features of real persons, and Fukuyama's piece is a caricature of serious argument. It is doubtful whether he has even read Hegel, whom he likes to quote by way of Kojève. He might have been embarrassed by Hegel's apotheosis of the Prussian state. Clearly, he knows little about the world today, and less about history. Nevertheless there is a case in his *aperçu* which is important, if only because it has become the implicit world view of many in both the 'capitalist' and the '(post-)communist' world. The view is simple, and it is wrong. It needs to be refuted and rejected.

Many people see the last forty years as a great battle between systems. The battle stretches back even further, to the Russian Revolution of 1917 perhaps, or indeed to the publication of *The Communist Manifesto* in 1848. It is the battle between communism and capitalism, between a socialist commonwealth and liberal democracy. For a long time, liberal capitalism was the stronger force; but in the course of this century the scales gradually tipped in favour of socialism/ communism. In the 1960s, it looked for a while as if the two systems would converge. To some extent this may have happened, but in the end another option prevailed. Both systems settled down in their mould and accepted the other in its own right. A truce was arranged which guaranteed the integrity of both. Perhaps it was called the Helsinki Final Act, though some would argue that the famous 'Third Basket' of Helsinki with its mention of human rights contained the seeds of upsetting the truce. In any case, the standoff did not last. Revolutionary processes took their course. One of the two systems looked increasingly shaky until it began to crumble and finally collapsed in 1989. After that, only one option is on offer, the capitalist option of liberal democracy.

Let me just make sure that I am not misunderstood: this is not my view of things, though it is that of many who find Fukuyama 'brilliant' and want to follow Hayek's extreme constitutionalism. Its fundamental mistake lies in the implicit or explicit understanding of the assumptions of American or British or German or French societies today as 'systems'. Paradoxically, if this understanding were correct, 'history' as Fukuyama sees it would still be with us. We would still be involved in a battle of systems. In fact, we are not. At any rate, we are not if the revolution of 1989 can retain its initial gains. For the common language which we speak today is not the language of the West which has now been adopted by the East; it is an intrinsically universal language which belongs to nobody in particular and therefore to everybody. The countries of East Central Europe have not shed their communist system in order to embrace the capitalist system (whatever that is); they have shed a closed system in order to create an open society, *the* open society to be exact, for while there can be many systems, there is only one open society. If any creed has won in the events of last year, it is the idea that we are all embarked on a journey into an uncertain future and have to work by trial and error within institutions which make it possible to bring about change without bloodshed. What has died in the streets of Prague and Berlin and Bucharest, in the endless meetings of Budapest, on your Round Table and now in your parliament, is not just communism, but the belief in a closed world which is governed by a monopoly of 'truth'.

François Furet has remarked to me that for the first time in 150 years, if not more, no alternative total view of society is on offer in the intellectual and political battles of the world. This means (I would add) that we can at last get down to the real business of history, which is to advance the life chances of men and women everywhere. The road to freedom is not a road from one system to another, but one that leads into the open spaces of infinite possible futures, some of which compete with each other. Their competition makes history. The battle of systems is an illiberal aberration. To drive the point home with the utmost force: if capitalism is a system, then it needs to be fought as hard as communism had to be fought. All systems mean serfdom, including the 'natural' system of a total 'market order' in which no one tries to do anything other than guard certain rules of the game discovered by a mysterious sect of economic advisers.

Mostly about the Strange Death of Socialism and the Mirage of a 'Third Way'

As I allow my enthusiasm for the open society to run away with rational argument, it occurs to me that you may be a little too pleased with some of my remarks.

You too have your doubts about Hayek, and you want some mixture of socialist achievements and liberal opportunities to prevail. Unbridled capitalism, you think, is not such a good thing, and you may therefore wish to enlist me as one of your supporters on the road to social democracy. I do not share the widespread obsession with labels and am therefore not particularly upset about being called a social democrat, though I have difficulties with the Italian epithet, *liberalsocialista*, because I prefer to think of myself as a radical liberal for whom the social entitlements of citizenship are as important a condition of progress as the opportunities for choice which require entrepreneurial initiative and an innovative spirit. But before we get to normal politics the point has to be made unequivocally that socialism is dead, and that none of its variants can be revived for a world awakening from the double nightmare of Stalinism and Brezhnevism.

Lest you think such language unnecessarily cruel, let me tell you about a book which has to do with my own political philosophy, George Dangerfield's *The Strange Death of Liberal England*, which first appeared in 1935. Dangerfield traces the curious story of the great triumph of the British Liberals under the Asquith ministry after 1908, and the hubris which led to their rapid decline from 1913 onwards. 'It was in these years that that highly moral, that generous, that dyspeptic, that utterly undefinable organism known as the Liberal Party died the death. It died from poison administered by its Conservative foes, and from disillusion over the inefficacy of the word "Reform". And the last breath which fluttered in this historical flesh was extinguished by War.' Dangerfield is not naive; he knows that political parties can appear to survive their death. 'I realise, of course, that the word "Liberal" will always have a meaning as long as there is one democracy left in the world, or any remnant of a middle class: but the true pre-war Liberalism – supported, as it still was in 1910, by Free Trade, a majority in Parliament, the ten commandments, and the illusion of Progress – can never return. It was killed, or killed itself, in 1913.' Dangerfield adds, for good measure, 'And a very good thing too.'

It is hard to resist the temptation to replace the year 1913 in these observations by 1989, and the word 'Liberalism' by 'socialism', or at any rate 'social democracy' – supported, as it still was in the 1970s, by economic planning, a majority in parliament, the creed of social service and the illusion of 'makeability'. But (you will point out immediately) is this not conflating two different things? There is socialism in its communist version – which collapsed dramatically in 1989 when country after country took the word out of its official description ('Socialist Republic of . . .'), and parties like your own, those of Hungary and even of Italy sought a less offensive label – and there is social democracy which if it died at all, 'perished in the dark' (thus Lord Selborne during the debate on the Parliament Act in 1911), unnoticed by many, because to all intents and purposes it is still very much around. Many other socialisms have cropped up in the last century and a half, but communism (which has also been described as 'really existing socialism' while it really existed) and social democracy (sometimes called, *pour épater le bourgeois*, 'democratic socialism') are the only two of any historical weight. Their story needs to be told, however briefly, in order to sort out what it means to speak of the strange death of socialism in the 1980s.

I suppose it all started in post-Napoleonic Europe, or more to the point, in the second phase of the industrial era, notably in England and France. Thoughtful people – bourgeois no doubt – were upset by the plight of the labouring classes and began to think of remedies. These had certain ingredients in common. One was that there was something wrong with the way in which private property had come to be used; to redress such wrongs, property had to be 'socialised' in one way or another. Another feature was that people's positions in society had become altogether too unequal; variants of egalitarianism accompanied socialism from its earliest days. The notion that things could, and had to be done by deliberate planning rather than left to their own resources, to the 'market', follows naturally. The cool rationality of such analyses was invariably coupled with more intangible and emotional hopes for a different way of living together, a sense of brotherly love, a desire to break the vicious cash nexus by voluntary co-operation and the spirit of solidarity. An alliance of intellectuals and the working class turned this mix into the vision of an altogether different world, Henri de Saint-Simon's 'New Christendom', Robert Owen's

40

'New Society'. Moreover, the new world had to be fought for by organising either islands of a better future or movements to transform the present.

Marx did not like these notions of the Saint-Simons and Owens, Cabets and Fouriers, Proudhons and Weitlings. He scorned the attempt to confront the miseries of the present with alternatives which were mere 'phantasies'. Instead, he invoked the inexorable march of History with a capital H. The New Society was not a desirable prospect but the necessary outcome of the contradictions and conflicts of bourgeois capitalism. This is where the notion of systems crept into socialism and allied itself with the Utopian vision which had been there all along. It does not matter what people want or visualise for themselves – indeed, people do not matter – for they merely execute the will of History, and History has chosen the proletariat to become the agent of productive forces which will overcome the capitalist mode of production and create the New Society, socialist first and communist when it has fully matured.

The parties formed in the name of *The Communist Manifesto* liked to threaten the powers that be with the inevitability of their downfall and the victory of socialism; but they were never strictly Marxist. It would actually be rather difficult to set up a trade union or a political party on the assumption that such movements are mere puppets of great impersonal forces. To have history on one's side – rather, to hear leaders tell one that this is the case – may sound encouraging to some, but an un-Marxian element of voluntarism crept into the socialist movement from the start. In England it was dominant from the Chartists to the Fabians and further to the Labour Party. With the formation of parties and a growing belief in their capacity to change things here and now, came social democracy; that is, the grudging yet sincere acceptance of the rules of the open society. Versions of positivism entered into a curious marriage with socialism. By 1914, liberalism may have died, but socialism was alive and kicking in the democracies of Europe, and its parliamentary representatives voted for the war loans of their respective governments just as proletarians of all countries went to war against each other instead of uniting behind the red flag.

1917 is not just another stage of the same story. While Lenin obviously belonged in the tradition to which I have alluded here with almost frivolous lightness, his success in Russia owes little if anything to the growth of social democracy in Europe, a great deal to uniquely Russian traditions and an important impetus to Marx. The reason for this particular debt is in many ways perverse, because it derives from an error of theory and of history which needs to be exposed. As you know, Marx tried to link the struggle of classes to underlying socioeconomic forces. The suppressed class draws its strength as well as its rhetoric from forces of production which are held back by the ruling class and from the mode of production which it represents. Marx needed this conflation of politics and economics to make the case for the inexorable march of History; but he had little history to go on. Some kind of class struggle had (perhaps) provided ammunition for the French Revolution; the Industrial Revolution can (probably) be described as the unavoidable removal of an older mode of production in order to make way for the new forces of technology, enterprise and wage labour. The two revolutions, however, did not happen in the same place or at the same time, except in the books of Marx and Engels, where the revolt of the Third Estate and the breakthrough of industrial production were superimposed by the strokes of two pens.

Marx was more interested in the revolution of the future than in those of the past. However, his theory in all its abstract splendour made little sense for this prospect either. The proletariat never represented a new force of production; it was a class of exploited and downtrodden industrial workers who needed to find a place in the sun of this world here and now. Marx himself was hard-pressed to identify the underlying socioeconomic force of the revolutionary movement which he tried to promote, for 'associated producers' and 'socialised ownership' are hardly compelling motives for change (especially if joint-stock companies are regarded as 'a necessary transitional point' on the road to socialism). Yet by a curious fluke, Marx's theory made sense for Russia. Indeed, it made sense for all countries which entered the modern world late, and had to achieve political and economic modernisation simultaneously and quickly. As older feudal or colonial elites were removed, those who took over could claim to do so in the name of hitherto repressed opportunities for economic growth. Contrary to the early English or American or French or Dutch bourgeoisie they had no past economic achievement or wealth to rely on, nor were they a *Bildungsbürgertum* in the German sense, an 'educated bourgeoisie' (to use a term by which Keynes described his own origins); instead, political power was the sole base of their position. Thus it came about that a class rose to hegemony which had nothing but the Party to support it, but which set in motion a slow and ultimately ineffectual process of industrialisation. 'Communism,' as Lenin put it crisply, 'is Soviet power plus the electrification of the whole country.'

Socialism of this brand – communism – is in other words a developing-country phenomenon. Despite some islands of sophistication and even of capitalism, Russia in 1917 was by and large a developing country in this sense. So was China in 1949, as were the many Third World nations which found it convenient to rely on the Soviet model, and on support by the older Second World nations to boot. *Nomenklatura* socialism – some call it 'administrative centralism' or even 'democratic centralism' – became the preferred mode of late modernisation.

It was, as we know today, not a very effective method. Its effectiveness remained largely confined to the destruction of the old authoritarian regime. This was accomplished with utter ruthlessness. The 'harvest of sorrow' in the Ukraine and beyond (to use Robert Conquest's description) and the Chinese

Cultural Revolution are two unforgettable and unforgivable examples, though Idi Amin and 'Emperor' Bokassa and Pol Pot and other Third World 'modernisers', often in the name of socialism, will not be forgotten or forgiven either. The destructive part of the process did lead to a certain levelling of inherited social hierarchies and the creation of the institutions (though often merely the trappings) of modern states. It also laid certain foundations of modern economic development, elements of infrastructure (though often more symbolic than useful), generalised education (though often for purposes of mobilisation as much as skilling), large industrial complexes (though often geared to state, above all military, purposes rather than consumer demand). But the process failed to do that crucial trick which the 'Protestant ethic' achieved in some parts of the Western world, that is, to provide an incentive for saving, and for that deferred gratification which is a condition of early industrial success. People must be prepared to allow an accumulation of capital which sets the growth machine in motion. They may do so voluntarily – because they believe it is morally right, or because they can see the light at the end of the tunnel – but if they do not, they must be compelled to consume less than they produce. This is how forced labour came to be an indispensable ingredient of really existing socialism, as well as shortages and queues and in the end a huge and useless 'overhang' of worthless money. The logic of communist regimes made exploitation and suppression as inevitable as scarcity and pretence.

The promise of socialism of the communist variety was a quick and painless way out of authoritarian rule and preindustrial poverty. Modernity without Napoleon and the gin houses, as it were. In fact, the peoples of the Third World including the Soviet Union got both, dictators and misery. Above all they got what Milovan Djilas first called a 'new class' of party officials. This class increasingly hardened into a large *nomenklatura*. The more rigid it became, the less sustainable was its rule. The combination of ineffectiveness and suppression eventually set in motion the process of self-destruction which we have watched in recent years. In other words, socialism is not only a developing-country phenomenon, but it is one which cannot be upheld beyond the initial stages of development. Sooner or later it has to give way to more open and effective modes of economic advancement and probably political involvement as well. Really existing socialism cannot last.

There are those in the Soviet Union and elsewhere in the post-communist world who speak today of a 'return to capitalism'. They are wrong in more ways than one, but above all in clinging to Marx's mistaken assumption that socialism succeeds capitalism. In fact, the opposite is the case. Market-oriented economies based on incentives rather than planning and force represent an advanced stage of modern development. In this sense, capitalism succeeds socialism – in those countries where the socialist option was the chosen method of entering the modern world. This is of course not the case in your country, let alone in East

Germany and Czechoslovakia, where really existing socialism was the result of the hegemonic aspirations of the Soviet Union and stunted the hopeful saplings of the process of modernisation. One can understand that, faced with the rubble left behind by the Second World War, large numbers of people were prepared to embrace any promise of progress on offer, including *nomenklatura* socialism, but after forty years the balance sheets of the regimes under its yoke show almost exclusively red figures. Soviet-style socialism in the advanced countries of East Central Europe was a tragedy without relief.

1917 had more than one effect. It established really existing socialism of the developing-country variety, but it also encouraged those in more developed countries who were unhappy about what they saw as the accommodation of socialist parties to the status quo, to remain on a more absolute course. Communist parties came into being which have played a horrific and often murderous part in the long-running battles with social democrats, notably in the Spanish Civil War, during the Hitler-Stalin Pact, and in some European countries during the immediate post-war period as well. When the Soviets forced the countries of your region under their rule by forming 'popular fronts', 'unity parties' or merely communist-dominated 'coalitions', they could rely on communist parties of varying but not inconsiderable strength. The fifth column was there to support their claims, and while the false god of communism failed most of its believers (as Arthur Koestler, Ignazio Silone, Stephen Spender

47

and others have told us), it failed too late and too slowly.

It is important to remember this nightmare from which we are waking up today. I remember it well because I was a young man in Berlin when the Russians came at the end of April 1945. Our family welcomed them warmly because I had been hiding for weeks after my unexpected release from the concentration camp in which I had spent the previous winter, and above all because we were waiting for my father, who was in prison for his involvement in the resistance and notably the plot to kill Hitler on 20 July 1944. Having seen his socialist friends murdered, he came back convinced that there must never be disunity in the labour movement again. At first, the communist leaders who had returned from their Soviet exile did not want to hear this message. They thought that they could go it alone, and in any case they did not like the social democrats, whom they had denounced as 'social fascists' a mere five years before. Within a year, attitudes turned full circle. Soon the communists realised that they would not win free elections; apart from the Italian city of Bologna, the Indian province of Kerala and one or two other places, communists have never won free elections anywhere; and so they put pressure on the social democrats to form a 'Socialist Unity Party'. By that time, my father, who never succumbed to the pressures or the temptations of totalitarianism of any ilk, had made up his mind. As Vice-Chairman of the Central Committee of the East German Social Democrats, he voted against the forced merger, and had to flee to the West. I confess that while *Schaden-freude* is not the most noble of emotions, I watched with some pleasure the disintegration of that miserable assemblage of privileged cowards which called itself the SED.

On all this, however, you probably agree. But what about the other, the social-democratic thread of developments since 1917? One key difference is now apparent. Whereas communism and really existing socialism engaged in their own constitutional politics and set up monopolies of unfettered Party power wherever they could, social democracy after 1917 became clearly and (except for some fringe groups) unambiguously a part of normal politics in the democracies of the world. Some thought that this was exactly what was wrong with it. It has to be admitted that Ramsay MacDonald and Hermann Müller and perhaps even Léon Blum were not the most inspiring leaders of political parties committed to radical reform. But it is also true that by involving themselves in normal politics, social democrats became staunch defenders of the constitution of liberty. Democracy and the rule of law were in good hands with them. As newcomers to its pastures they showed if anything a greater commitment to the values and institutions of the open society than older liberals.

So what went wrong? Did anything go wrong? You reminded me of the article I wrote a few years ago called 'The Misery of Social Democracy', which obviously caused you some heartache. (In this you are not alone; Willy Brandt, in his farewell speech as leader

49

of the West German Social Democrats, expressed pained bewilderment: 'I have asked myself time and again which decades those contemporaries had in mind who thought that the social democratic century is over. Have they overlooked the two wars, fascism and Stalinism, the great economic crises and the new existential threats?') At the time, I started with the straightforward observation that social democratic parties all over Europe were not doing very well, and those who were doing well, like those of Spain and perhaps Italy, were not particularly social democratic. Advocating a decent society was evidently no longer good enough for the electorate of advanced societies. What had brought about this change of fortunes for the dominant political force of a century?

The simplest answer is, victory. Like the British Liberals in 1911, social democrats had conquered Europe by the end of the 1970s. Their combination of democracy and planning, of economic freedom and demand management, of individual choice and redistribution, of liberty and justice, had become the dominant reality of the OECD world (though the United States went partly its own way and never fully recognised the social rights of citizenship). We were all social democrats then, and in important respects we still are.

For the people of the developed world, this was fine, but for social democracy it was fatal. The creation of a large majority of those who could hope to satisfy many of their aspirations within existing conditions – a majority class – made social democratic parties either a protective, not to say conservative, force, or dispensable, or both. The emergence of a majority class (sometimes called a middle class, though the concept is misleading in the absence of an upper class which sets the tone, and a cohesive working class) meant above all that the traditional social base of social democracy had melted away. The working class had disappointed its intellectual leaders; contrary to their assumptions, it was actually not a particularly progressive social force, but one that sought 'law and order' as much as social and economic advancement, and whose members were in the end quite pleased to make it for themselves and their families, never mind all the others. Class conflict was transformed into individual social mobility. The prevalence of this pattern in America in the form of the 'American dream', if not always its reality, has often been cited as the reason for the absence of socialist parties in that country; now the same behaviour began to spread in Europe. As the process went on, the working class not only lost its cohesion, but began to shrink. A new middle class of white-collar employees emerged, and while their market position may have seemed similar to that of workers, they never saw themselves as a part of the proletariat. This shift from manufacturing to services reduced the industrial working class to a minority, and one whose status could no longer be described as neglected or downtrodden.

The crumbling traditional base of social democratic parties was accompanied by another effect of their victory. Social democracy has had a peculiar affinity to the state. Far from fighting it as the 'body which administers the common business interests of the bourgeois class' (in Marx's and Engels' formulation), social democrats used it to redress the injustices of capitalism. John Maynard Keynes and William Beveridge were both Liberals by party affiliation, but Keynesian economic policy and Beveridge-type social policy became hallmarks of social democracy. 'Policy' always means a greater role for government. This in turn led to the expansion of the planning apparatus, of bureaucracy. Social democracy became increasingly associated with bureaucracy, to the point where, in some countries such as Sweden, it turned into the party of public servants. Elsewhere it has been described as the 'teachers' party' (teachers being public servants in most European countries) or the 'party of local government employees', which amounts to the same thing.

The quandary is evident. While there may still be much to do in order to complete the social-democratic project, its traditional support has dwindled as a consequence of its success. Moreover, the link of social democracy with bureaucracy puts the old reformist force into a strange predicament. After all, bureaucracy is in a sense the democratic *nomenklatura* which, if we follow Max Weber's fears, may yet imprison us all in a new 'cage of bondage'. One aspect of the 1980s in the OECD world is the protest not only against the economic stagflation of the 1970s but also against the political dependence on bureaucracy. People have an elementary desire to do things their way rather than be pushed about by characters in offices who make them fill in forms and wait in queues for unsatisfactory answers.

I realise, of course, that the phrase 'social democratic' will always have a meaning as long as there is one democracy left in the world, or any remnant of a working class. This is paraphrasing Dangerfield yet again, but so far as the working class is concerned, I am not even sure it is true. The remaining working class is by no means a safe reservoir for social-democratic votes. Anyway, social democracy is in trouble, and it is in trouble at the very time at which more absolute versions of socialism have run aground. Does this mean (you asked me) that the social democratic option is foreclosed for those who have abandoned communism?

The time has come to face squarely one issue which vitiates much of the debate about democratisation in Europe. It has somewhat awkward names, all of which aim at describing a halfway house between the realities of what used to be the West and what used to be the East. Some speak of a 'middle way', some of a 'third way', and all believe that it would be wrong to shed the achievements of forty years of socialism and swallow capitalism lock, stock and barrel. Surely – you seemed to say when we talked – there must be a place for a decent social and democratic, or even democratic socialist policy somewhere in between the extremes of what you had and what we have. This sounds good, even plausible, yet it is the wrong way to approach the tasks which lie ahead both in theory and in practice.

Instead of taking up Milovan Djilas, Ota Sik, Rudolf Bahro, or other writers from socialist countries, or the great advocate of humane capitalism in the 1960s and 1970s, Andrew Shonfield, let me use a Swiss author to make my case. In January 1990 the said author wrote a calm and reasoned article in the liberal *Neue Zürcher Zeitung* on 'the possibility of a third way for Eastern Europe'. He cautions the West against the self-important arrogance of the view that the collapse of really existing socialism leaves no alternative to its victims but to adopt all features of democratic and capitalist market economies on the grounds that one cannot be 'a little pregnant'. The author reminds us of the 'pure doctrine of capitalism': self-organisation, private property, the market, reliable rules of the game. He adds that the reality of the West is often far from this doctrine, and makes a number of points. Private property has changed its complexion in giant enterprises which are run by people who do not own them; at the other end, small family-owned firms are by no means a model of efficiency. Planning and market forces have long ceased to be incompatible; the real question is where to draw the boundary between the two. Transparent cost and price structures are a good idea, but very far from the murky reality of the 'markets' for agricultural products, or the labour 'market'. The free movement of people, or even of goods, is as much a promise as it is a reality. 'Let us not be more Popish than the Pope,' he counsels.

So far so good. But the author then links his observations with a plea for 'utopian visions' which 'transcend systems'. There is much space for reform everywhere (he argues), and the analogy to being 'a little pregnant' is a misleading description of economic structures in view of the need to seek complex mixtures of elements. This need has to be explored 'across the systems without ideological prejudice and self-important arrogance. Liberal and socialist Utopias might thus be turned into a synergetic third.' The 'socialist Utopia' could be enriched by entrepreneurial initiative, and the 'capitalist Utopia' by the insight that the economy serves human beings, and not vice versa. Thus we should begin 'the kind of inter-cultural dialogue which might lead to a variegated and dynamic path to Central Europe.'

No, is the simple answer to this demand. We should not engage in this 'inter-cultural dialogue', and more, the very idea needs to be quashed. It is wrong because it is another version of system thinking, and thinking in terms of systems lies at the bottom of illiberty in all its varieties. It is no accident that our author uses notions like 'transcending systems', or exploring ideas 'across the systems'. This is how he sees the world. The only difference to, say, Fukuyama is that he wants to introduce a third system, 'Central Europe' as it were, halfway between socialism and capitalism. (I know that you like the notion of Central Europe because you do not want to be labelled East European; indeed Poland has set its clocks to Central European Time throughout all these years and against Soviet pressure as well as the logic of geography; but the concept is nonetheless laden with ideological baggage

– especially in its German incarnation, which brings back the 'national socialist' Friedrich Naumann and his *Mitteleuropa* as well as other unsavoury characters – so let us be careful in using it!) Our Swiss author fortunately calls the system 'variegated' but is nevertheless taken in by its 'Utopian' qualities. His is a kind of Rousseauean Utopia in which the 'ritual competition between majority-forming pseudo-alternatives' is replaced by 'committed discussions of political programmes' and of course, a good dose of 'human warmth, empathy and solidarity'.

We must beware of Utopia too, not only if it is of the Rousseauean variety. Utopia is in the nature of the idea a total society. It may exist 'nowhere' but it is held as a counter-project against the realities of the world in which we are living. Utopia is a complete alternative, and therefore of necessity a closed society. Why did I not write the planned anti-Orwell book, *Nineteen Eighty-nine*? Because I could not find a way out of Big Brother's *Nineteen Eighty-four* for Winston Smith. Benevolent Utopias are no better. Karl Popper's demolition of Plato's *Republic* has precisely this theme. Whoever sets out to implement Utopian plans will in the first instance have to wipe clean the canvas on which the real world is painted. This is a brutal process of destruction. Second, a new world will have to be constructed which is bound to lead to errors and failures, and will in any case require awkward transitional periods like the 'dictatorship of the proletariat'. The probability must be high that in the end we will be stuck with the transition; dictators are not in the habit of giving up their power. The Utopian, writes Popper, 'may seek his heavenly city in the past or in the future; [he] may preach "back to nature" or "forward to a world of love and beauty"; but [the] appeal is always to our emotions rather than to reason. Even with the best intentions of making heaven on earth it only succeeds in making it a hell – that hell which man alone can prepare for his fellow-men.'

All this applies to the Utopia of the middle way as it does to all others. As a complete 'third system' it remains primarily a system, never mind the 'third' or 'fourth' or 'fifth'. In the conflicts between advocates of systems and defenders of the open society it therefore belongs on the side of illiberty where all systems have their place. Neither Central Europe nor social democracy nor any other euphemism for the 'middle way' must be thought of as a system, or indeed a Utopia, if liberty is what we want. The choice between freedom and serfdom is stark and clear, and it offers no halfway house for those weaker souls who would like to avoid making up their minds.

All this time, we have been talking constitutional politics, of course. It is therefore necessary to define more precisely the ingredients of the open society. Since at this stage the issue is social and economic, we must ask which elements of economic organisation are constituent parts of the open society and which others can be left to normal politics. Capitalism has often been defined in this context. Most definitions contain three elements: *private actors* co-ordinate their economic activity through the *market* in order to achieve accumulation and *growth*. How much of this is a part of the definition of an open society?

The question is extraordinarily difficult to answer, but it is undoubtedly a legitimate subject of debate and we can have a go at it. Take property. John Locke and his contemporaries would have had no doubt that private property is a constitutional requirement. Indeed it probably is, though that does not mean that all property has to be private. State-owned railways are perfectly compatible with the open society. The key is that private property must be available as an option, and it must be protected. Then there is the market. It has many implications, some constitutional and some not. Without legally protected contracts there can be no market; this is a constitutional need. Monopolies restrict the market, though this raises, even apart from the railways, the question of 'natural monopolies' – for example, of air and of water. It is a constitutional condition of the open society that the generalisation of monopolies be prevented. The burden of proof must always be on the defender of monopoly rather than on the advocate of pluralism and competition. Further, accumulation and growth. One ancient open society, Great Britain, has experienced many decades of indifferent or even 'negative' growth without becoming illiberal. One can understand those who worry that economic growth may have become an almost constitutional postulate in a number of countries. Harold James has made the point for Germany, where 'economic advance' has only too often in the last two centuries appeared to be the purpose 'without which the nation could not exist'. The constitutional requirement in this respect probably lies with the availability of incentives. Freedom to choose one's profession, freedom of movement, and arguably limits to the progression of taxation belong in this category.

This is to say that neither demand management *à la* Keynes nor social security *à la* Beveridge are constitutionally incompatible with an open society. Indeed, many economic patterns which no textbook would describe as capitalist exist in democracies. The Japanese economy is hardly capitalist, with its large companies and their organised relations within the Ministry of International Trade and Industry. In Germany the role of the big banks, and of an informal network of major employers and trade unionists, coupled with co-determination and a highly developed welfare state, is hardly compatible with the publicly professed market economy. Sweden is in no strict sense a capitalist country. Yet these and others with their own idiosyncrasies are – with reservations in the case of Japan – open societies. The constitutional prerequisites of democracy are present.

The examples suggest an answer to your questions (and to the Utopian visions of the Swiss author whom, for the sake of clarity, I have perhaps treated a little harshly). There do exist aspects of economic order which belong to the constitution of liberty. They are, as it were, non-negotiable. In your own country, as in others under communist domination, some of them were absent. There was no law of contract. There was instead a near-total state monopoly. Private property was absent or severely restricted. Basic economic freedoms were missing. Without any 'inter-cultural dialogue' aimed at compromise and a mishmash of systems, these missing elements of the open society will have to be established if liberty is to stay. Like the common language which we speak again, such elements are neither East nor West nor Central European, but universal prerequisites of freedom.

Then there is normal politics. If you want your country to be not only a home of free speech and political choice, but a place of prosperity and economic opportunity, I strongly recommend many of the liberal policies which your courageous Minister of Finance Balcerowicz – or his Czech counterpart Vaclav Klaus, and some others elsewhere – are pursuing. Some elements of this policy border on the constitutional, but most are the legitimate subject of political debate and therefore of divergent views. American-style capitalism is only one way forward; few others anywhere in the world have opted for it. Britain may have displayed some similar traits in an earlier phase of modern economic development, but the two reformers whom I like to quote, Keynes and Beveridge, were after all British, and of Keynes it has been said that he saved capitalism by destroying it. The economic structures of France and Germany, of Italy and Spain, of the Netherlands and Sweden are different in dozens of significant respects. There is no Central European model; there are as many models as there are countries.

Thus the notion of a third, or middle, way is not only wrong in theory because it arouses the totalitarian potential of all Utopias; it is also wrong in practice. In constitutional terms, there are only two ways: we have to choose between systems and the open society. In terms of normal politics, there are a hundred ways, and we can forever learn from one another in framing our own – your own, my own, everybody's, or at least every country's own – pattern of economic and social progress. None of these patterns is a model for others, let alone a system. Reality is infinitely varied. It may be a nightmare for the conceptual purist, but this must not mislead us to sanctify it into a system. As long as the constitution of liberty is safe and sound, real people thrive in a real world for which all tidy concepts are inappropriate.

One other point needs to be made, although it is painful. The Swiss author rightly warned against arrogance on the part of those of us who were fortunate enough to live in conditions of liberty and prosperity while your people were suffering the leaden hand of *nomenklatura* socialism. His laudable compassion led him, as it does many others, to demand that the 'achievements' of forty years of socialism be preserved even as its errors are undone. But what are these achievements? In terms of constitutional politics, I am afraid that I cannot see any. The much-quoted social rights embodied in your constitutions are not worth the paper on which they are written. No constitutional 'right to work' can prevent unemployment; all it does is to discredit the constitution because it promises something which no judge can provide. A policy of full employment may rank high among the priorities of normal politics, but an article in the constitution is no substitute for it. (The right not to work is a more plausible candidate for constitutional guarantee, because it protects people against forced labour.) Nor can I see much in the field of normal politics that one would wish to preserve in the formerly socialist countries.

Something else remains, on which you placed great emphasis in our conversation. It has to do with the deep sense of loss felt by some in the post-communist world because it appears that a style of life is irretrievably passing away which had much to recommend it. It was a less hectic style than that of the 'capitalist' West, more sociable, more concerned with cultural values than the materialistic hedonism of the consumer society permits. You were quite specific on this point. It was right, you said, to subsidise good films rather than rent out video porn, indeed to make sure that cheap books of value (you said 'classical' books) are available to everybody. I appreciate your intentions but cannot follow your conclusions. To some extent, people's predilection for culture in totalitarian regimes is a substitute for other values which they are denied. Once the pressure lifts, they go for tabloids and hamburgers and dishwashers and shiny motorcycles and holidays on the Costa Brava. It would be nice if some of the less shallow values could be preserved, but it is hard to see how this can be done. I suspect that even if your government continued to subsidise 'good' films and 'classical' books, people will prefer to see cheap romance and read trash, or no longer read at all.

The reason is simple, and important in this context. As one looks at our world from a distance, one would like to see the objectives in which one believes, achieved directly and without detour or distraction. Perhaps what you call social democracy is an example of such an objective. But short of the horror of a 'benevolent' dictatorship, this is not the way the world works. At least, open societies do not work that way. Whether we like it or not, the pendulum's swing from one side to the other – and it need not swing all the way from one extreme to the other – is the more likely rhythm of change. After the victory of social democracy in the OECD world, people wanted a new splurge of individualism, of innovation and initiative, and of consumerism. They elected Margaret Thatcher Prime Minister of Britain, and Ronald Reagan President of the United States and even their 'socialist' leaders like the Prime Ministers of Spain and Australia and New Zealand turned out to be what some called 'left Thatcherites'.

Now, at the beginning of the 1990s, the time may have come for us to turn back from the provisions party to the entitlements party, that is, from obsession with economic growth to recognition of the requirements of citizenship. Even the Republican President of the United States has promised a 'kinder, gentler America', and in Europe the change of mood is unmistakable.

At the same time, it would not be surprising if your

compatriots and your neighbours want to have their share of Western individualism, including consumerism and all that, before they remember the social needs of those who will be left behind. Some may regret this, but it is the price you pay for decades of glum and grey collectivism. I wish you well in your attempt to stem the tide of trash and glitter, but I suspect that it will sweep you away. Yours will be a minority position for a while, and as you undoubtedly perceive, I do not feel very sorry for you. At least, I do not feel sorry as long as the swing of the pendulum remains contained by the limits of the open society. In practice, this means that it must be possible to vote Balcerowicz out of office (not too soon, I hope; in eight years' time perhaps) and replace him by a more social democratic politician.

This takes me back again to your question of political parties and their social base. Who is going to support what in the years to come? What political structures are going to emerge from the collapse of the communist monopoly? The question has vexing dimensions, for while it is clear that the party systems of the European democracies, and of North America for that matter, would sit uneasily on the post-communist countries, your predicament reminds us of the fact that our own parties are out of date and out of tune with the times. The German experience has made the point perfectly. While West German parties have gone to great lengths and expense to restructure the numerous East German movements and sects along their lines, no fewer than thirteen groupings are represented in the freely elected parliament, and in many cases it is difficult to make sense of them either in terms of their programmes or their electoral support.

One wonders whether, if we were in your position and had to build our party structures in the old democracies from scratch, the same would happen here. Along with class conflict, the two-party system has crumbled. Everywhere, new groups seek a place among the old. Many of these are social movements, like the Greens, or one-issue parties, like the Five-Sixths Party in Luxemburg (which demands five-sixths of people's final income for pensioners). Some try to cut across traditional divisions, like the Alliance in Britain, now called Social and Liberal Democrats. In the United States, it has been observed that politics is now conducted by 536 entrepreneurs, 435 Representatives, 100 Senators and one President. (The cynic might add that members of the House have a 'turnover' of $1 million per election, members of the Senate $10 million and the President $100 million.) You were thus quite right to raise the question of party after class, and I am not sure that my answer will satisfy you.

In your country, of course, as in others in the post-communist world, you still have some way to go in order to join the great social-democratic consensus. I suspect that if developments in East Central Europe remain undisturbed from outside, or from antidemocratic forces within, the pendulum of normal politics will have to swing once in the liberal and once in the social direction before you feel that you have made it. The liberal direction means of course Balcerowicz if not Friedman (though I hope not Hayek); it involves the jump start of economies whose batteries have been flat for a very long time, with I hope the more fortunate countries of Europe and North America providing the lead to the necessary energy. The next steps can be taken in a variety of ways; *perestroika* too has as many variants as there are countries and organised views within them. They range from monetary union in Germany to massive privatisation in Hungary. All of these steps will – and should – be taken as a part of the initial momentum of constitutional change, that is, before there are fully formed political parties. Opposition to this process is bound to arise, and it will be about the social cost of economic growth. At some point, in four or even eight years' time (how I hope that you will have this time for reform which must seem endless and threatening now!), other groups will take over. They may even be called social democrats.

All the while, however, our own problem will be a lingering reality for you as well. Here, the forces for change are fragmented and often weak. On the one hand, the place of class has been taken by what some have called 'disparities of realms of life'. This means that all of us have certain interests in common in one of our 'realms of life', like the integrity of the physical environment, whereas we may have divergent interests in other 'realms of life', like the distribution of wealth. Thus trade unionists and employers can both be 'green' at times, but they remain on opposite sides of the table when it comes to wage settlements. Special interests, and social movements built around them, take the place of political parties; individuals no longer 'belong' to one group which combines most of their concerns, but they switch allegiances depending on the priority of one or other theme at different times. We have not yet invented institutions to accommodate this change. Not only parties but parliaments too were built around the idea of the class struggle, with the 'right' and the 'left' in their respective places if not on opposite sides. In any case, as you sit down to think about the rules of the game of your political process, you will wish to take the facts of conflict after class into account. Here, too, *The Federalist Papers* are relevant, not least because the US Constitution was never constructed or applied to accommodate class cleavages in the European way.

The other force for change is even more problematic, and you may not like it at all. It consists of active minorities of people who have thought about things and have advice to give to those who are in a position to act on such advice. You probably do not regard yourself as an intellectual, but I am one. I can therefore see that the demise of socialism not only has many practical consequences and raises questions such as those which you asked, but it also threatens the very existence of a group which has played a major role in the recent history of Europe. Perhaps intellectuals are not a group; they are a gaggle, a motley assortment, a category at best, but many of them have had a special affinity to socialism. Socialism was an intellectual invention, from Saint-Simon to Lassalle, from Marx to Gramsci, and through the hundreds of byways of Marxism which are now all ending in the sewers of discarded history.

One influential posture of intellectuals in Europe over the last hundred years had three ingredients. (In a half-hearted way they are still present among the bureaucratised intelligentsia in the universities and the media.) One was the outright rejection of present conditions as endemically rotten and incapable of repair. The second was a more or less elaborate vision of a totally different world in which the ills of reality are remedied. And the third was a great sense of certainty about both the rejection and the vision. Alienation, utopia and dogmatism do not form a very attractive triad, though it is one which leads almost naturally to versions of socialism which are not of the social-democratic variety.

I say this without any sense of delight or superiority. After all, I grew up in this world, and have feelings of friendship for some of those who manage to combine their socialist certainties with a personal decency which belies their creed. One or two have even turned out to be reliable 'constitutional patriots' without abandoning their claims to the rejection of the present and a utopian future. I feel much more alien among the new 'intellectuals' of the right, notably among those who have embraced an unconditional and often vicious defence of Thatcherism with the same total devotion which they once gave to socialism and even communism. It is true that in recent years the unusual has happened, and *der Geist weht rechts*, creative minds have espoused right-wing causes. Some of these are of lasting importance. While John Rawls may survive Robert Nozick and others who were prepared to shed 'justice as fairness' in favour of the 'minimal state', public choice theorists and constitutional economists have a great deal to offer when it comes to the issues with which I am dealing in this letter. But having said that, there remain the many for whom the demise of socialism means that a chasm has opened up, a great vacuum which is as disconcerting emotionally as intellectually. They no longer know where to go, and like the Italian Communist Party (of blessed memory) or the magazine *Marxism Today* in Britain they combine a courageous preparedness for change with a remarkable confusion of ideas.

Some of these doubly homeless intellectuals – 'free-floating' in any case and now robbed of their socialist mental home as well – try to keep a dream of some 'real' socialism alive. They claim that none of the really existing versions had anything to do with the real thing; indeed, they were all betrayals of the true socialist ideal. They speak of 'socialism with a human face', but the attempt is pathetic and will not lead anywhere. Kjell-Olof Fjeldt, social democrat and former Swedish minister of finance, has put it succinctly: 'If it is that difficult to give a concept a human face, I want nothing to do with it.' I would recommend to those who still cannot get socialism out of their minds an intellectual tradition which is admittedly less impressive in numbers, but includes some upright individuals who have proved immune to the temptations of dogma and utopian fantasies when these were strong. Karl Popper belongs squarely in this tradition. So does Raymond Aron, and perhaps Norberto Bobbio. John Maynard Keynes and William Beveridge have a place in this gallery. Max Weber can be found in it despite his early forays into nationalist pastures. The authors of the *Federalist*, Alexander Hamilton, John Jay and James Madison, were not tempted by tyranny, and likewise belong in this tradition (although I wonder what they would have said about being called intellectuals). And there are others, fortunately. They are all children of Kant, and of Hume and Locke before him, but emphatically not of Hegel or even of Rousseau. They are passionate defenders of the open society and at the same time committed reformers. One would be hard-pressed to place them on the left-right spectrum which the French Revolution has bequeathed us. Keynes put it well. He could not be a Conservative – 'I should not be amused or excited or edified'. He could not be a socialist because he worried about 'the party which hates existing institutions and believes that great good will result merely from overthrowing them'. Rather, he wrote, 'I incline to believe that the Liberal Party is still the best instrument of future progress – if only it had strong leadership and the right programme.' Today, the liberal *party* is just as likely to be a minority of active reformers who believe in the constitution of liberty.

All this is in some sense by the way, more to amuse

you than to answer your questions. Perhaps it helps to explain why I am so sceptical about social democracy, and also about the third way. My own liberal position is that of a constitutional liberalism which in the realm of normal politics advocates radical reform. I want to see entitlements of citizenship raised as well as the spirit of innovation and entrepreneurship aroused. Naturally, I believe that this is a helpful position both in your predicament and in ours. Communism has collapsed; social democracy is exhausted. We may have to live for some time with the shells of yesterday's politics, whatever their name may be. Thus you will probably adopt the labels of political parties familiar from the older democracies. But the old politics is spent. Constitutional liberalism and social reform need to build a new alliance. This is neither just your problem nor merely ours; it is a European problem which we have to resolve together.

Mostly about Politics, Economics and the Road to Freedom

It is quite clear, then, what the people in the new democracies want to get away from, and fairly clear where they want to get to, but how one finds one's way from socialism to the open society remains a wide open question. Many have commented on the surprising dearth of answers to it. We have several attempts to explain the rise of capitalism since the sixteenth century, and industrialism since the eighteenth, and some accounts of the emergence of democracy in America and in England, but they are of limited relevance to countries which have much less time and in any case operate under very different conditions if only because the others have gone before them. We have a considerable number of theories predicting the imminent downfall of capitalism and the inevitable rise of socialism – they include Marx's *Communist Manifesto* as well as Hayek's *The Road to Serfdom* – but today we know that they are all wrong. We have no theories which could help us bring about, or even understand, the transition from socialism to the open society. Perhaps this too is an aspect of the great *trahison des clercs*: intellectuals have explained events which never took place, and shied away from those which lie behind the revolution of '89 in Europe.

The issue is how to establish the constitution of liberty and anchor it firmly. The heart of the problem lies in the incongruent time scales of the political, the economic and the social reforms needed to this end. You tended to skirt this problem a little, if I may say so. Perhaps you were too taken in by the apparent continuity of political change in Poland, and also by the evident strength of certain elements of civil society, notably the Church and Solidarity. It is true that others were not as fortunate; President Havel has to rely on his enthusiastic artist friends and on the good sense, even humour of the Czech and Slovak people; in Romania the vacuum is frightening and it attracts all kinds of powers, old and new. But the apparent continuity of Poland is also deceptive, not only because it concealed the fragmentation of parties for a while, but above all because the problem of political, economic and social time is real everywhere.

When I say that there is no theory which could help us understand the current transition, I am not unaware of the growing number of books and conferences in which your story is compared to those of Southern Europe, Latin America and Southeast Asia. The Harvard political scientist Samuel Huntington (whom you know because you met him when we met in March) has invoked an even more sweeping context for current developments. He detects great waves of democratisation, followed by reverses. One such wave lasted from the American 1820s to the First World War in Europe and was reversed in the inter-war period. A second wave followed the Allied victory in the Second World War, though from the early 1960s onwards some of its gains were undone. A third wave started in Southern Europe and Latin America in the mid 1970s, then spread to Asia and finally to Eastern Europe. Huntington observes that 'all in all, apart from Eastern Europe, two dozen countries shifted from strictly authoritarian regimes to primarily democratic ones during the fifteen years after 1974 and in 1989 about 50 countries had some form of democratic institutions.'

Was it just the infectiousness of democracy which caused the process? Huntington places much emphasis on a modicum of 'economic wealth' as a condition of democratisation, though he adds external factors (Gorbachev) and internal developments ('legitimacy decay') to his list. He also adds a warning. Consolidation becomes plausible only after a country has passed the 'two-turnover test', that is, two changes of the political complexion of government by elections; and long before that, *el desencanto* is likely to set in, disenchantment with the slowness of progress and the inability of democracies to cope.

Such analogies and generalisations are helpful; yet in at least one respect Eastern Europe is different from the Latin countries of Europe and America and from Asia. None of them had to cope with the same near-total monopoly of a Party over state, economy and society. In the communist world, the three were indeed almost indistinguishable. There was no such thing as society, or an economy, or indeed the state; there was only the Party pervading everything else. In the Latin countries, on the other hand, the more typical picture was one of relatively thriving unsocial market economies protected by authoritarian dictatorships which left alone those who were prepared to withdraw to their private niches, but clamped down on any sign of active or even passive opposition. This was also the case in the Philippines and South Korea, and perhaps elsewhere in Asia. The Portuguese 'revolution of carnations' may sound as appealing as the Czechoslovak 'velvet revolution', but in fact the notion of revolution is much more applicable to Eastern Europe, where the all-encompassing claims of the ruling *nomenklatura* had to be broken.

Revolutions, however, are never very helpful for economic progress. Economies need confidence based on stable expectations, and such stability is the first victim of revolutionary upheavals. At the level of individual lives, they upset the routine of everyday experience and involve people in rare but costly excitements of history, demonstrating on Wenceslas Square, clambering through the first gaps in the Berlin Wall, watching the hated dictator lose his countenance and joining in the chants, 'Down with Ceauçescu.' All this happens on ordinary weekdays, when most should be in their factories or offices or even classrooms (though students can miss their lectures at less cost, which is one reason why they have played such a major part in recent upheavals). All normal priorities are set aside. People go hungry without even noticing, and they make do with less sleep than they ever thought possible. Once the excitement is over, they find it difficult to settle down to the old routine; and of course the excitement does not exactly increase productivity or production.

At the political level the temptation is great to begin with constitutional change. Nor is this just a temptation; the need is clear if the monopoly is to be broken. Your Round Table was not, and could not be a forum for normal politics, nor could it make decisions about the economy or issues of social policy. It was about constitutional politics, and that means the rules of the game. They are, as I have argued and shall argue again, a necessary condition of the road to freedom, but they are not a sufficient condition. When the French Revolution had taken its final turn for the worse, and people were rioting because they had nothing to eat, an angry Robespierre addressed the

Convention. 'What is this,' he said, 'they have the Republic and they cry for bread? Only tyrants give bread to their subjects. What the Constitution owes to the French people is freedom, cemented by humane laws. It is the enjoyment of the sacred rights of humanity and the exercise of all the social virtues that the Republic develops.' Gorbachev, fortunately, is no Robespierre, and Robespierre hardly stands for freedom and humane laws, but one can hear the President of the Soviet Union utter a similar sigh: What is this, they have free speech and elections and they moan about empty shelves in the shops? Man certainly does not live by bread alone, but neither does he, or she, live by *glasnost* and *perestroika*, or even democracy, alone.

Let me not pursue the story of the French Revolution all the way to *el desencanto* and beyond, at least not yet. If dire predictions of gloom were the only answer to your questions, it would be better to suffer in silence. What we are facing here is one of the more vexing issues of modern history, which is the relationship between political and economic reform, with social change thrown in at both ends. Clearly there is no simple answer. Deng Xiaoping may have hoped that he could stimulate economic activity at the local level and beyond without awakening the goddess of democracy. The students of Tiananmen Square gave him the answer, and his counterblast destroyed economic initiative along with demands for political participation. Mikhail Gorbachev may have hoped that he could release economic forces by lifting political

76

pressure. Once people were free to speak, to learn from abroad, to form co-operatives, even to make a little money, they would grasp their new opportunities and put the Soviet economy on a sustained path of growth (or so he thought). In fact, little happened, and worse, economic conditions deteriorated while political reform became more hectic. Ever new constitutional changes were thrown at an electorate which increasingly wanted bread rather than the Republic. The conflict may yet be the undoing of a great experiment of change.

Nor are the dilemmas of Deng and Gorbachev the only problems raised by the relationship of political and economic reform. Even if a country succeeds, as Poland did in August 1989, in bringing to power a new government which commands the respect of the people, and embarks on an economic course intended to stimulate initiative and create market conditions, a highly explosive predicament is bound to arise. It has to do with time scales, as I mentioned earlier. Basic constitutional changes can be introduced in a matter of months. They are, moreover, at least at first sight, a pure gain for all except the old *nomenklatura*, whom everybody wants to lose anyway. (Some will make the turning and survive, no doubt, and remain a simmering source of angry feelings of revenge.) Basic economic changes cannot be introduced in a matter of months. At any rate, they will not become effective immediately. On the contrary, economic reforms will without fail lead through a valley of tears. Things are bound to get worse before they get better. Even if a determined policy brings goods to the shops and creates a currency of real value without black market exchange rates, there will be many who earn too little to afford the goods, if they are employed at all. It is hard to tell how long the trek through the valley will take, but certain that it will take longer than the lifetime of the first parliament and always likely that it will engender a degree of disillusionment which will threaten the new constitutional framework along with the economic reforms, which promised so much but could not deliver in time.

I find those too cynical who argue with George Schoepflin that 'Western democracies have as one of their central characteristics the primacy of material interests and this is crucial in structuring the political game in such a way as to ensure a high degree of stability.' In fact, the two countries which I know best refute his claim. German democracy remains unstable precisely because it is so closely linked to material prosperity. Even the liberated East Germans were looking, it seems, for lolly as much as for liberty. A sense of institutions is missing, and when economic fortunes take a turn for the worse, one must fear for the constitution of liberty. British democracy, on the other hand, has remained quite stable through a long period of at least relative economic decline. It has remained unaffected by the temptations of totalitarianism despite people's worries in the 1920s that they had won the war but lost the peace, and despite the fact that Britain almost missed out on the economic miracle after the Second World War. It undoubtedly helps if democratic institutions and economic welfare flourish together, but once again there is no necessary relationship between the two, and above all no simple method of guaranteeing both.

What then is to be done? You have asked so many questions about the condition which I have described that for once I shall try to give you a fairly systematic, if unduly general reply and indicate three processes which are required in parallel on the road to freedom. Behind the scheme lies a methodological assumption (as one might almost call it) which has to do with the open society. There is no necessary, inescapable path to freedom, nor is there a royal road ahead. What is suggested here is imperilled and can fail at every stage. Freedom does not just happen, it has to be created. Moreover, its creation is full of pitfalls and surprises; in the end it will probably come about in much less systematic ways than any map of its route suggests. It also takes a good deal of luck to reach the destination. If adverse forces issue from the stars, or the neighbours, if the right people fail to come up at the right time, if inevitable small mistakes turn out to have uncontrollably large consequences, much may be lost. But as we think about the course of the human endeavour, we cannot just visualise a sinister road to serfdom; there is the prospect of a road to freedom as well.

Its first stage is about the constitution. This is the hour of the lawyers. By that of course I do not mean the litigious advocates of American courts, nor the philologists of arcane texts in the Roman law tradition, but those who have the imagination and comparative experience to find a way out of the monopoly of the Party and all subordinate monopolies too. This is the core issue, and it is not enough simply to remove the relevant article from existing constitutions.

A number of requirements come to mind. They are listed here without claim to completeness. Basic rights have to be promulgated. There are of course plenty of conventions and bills of rights which did not prevent Stalin from killing millions and the *nomenklatura* in all communist countries from arbitrarily arresting and torturing people, from censoring all publications, from stopping people travelling and choosing their employment, or from curtailing other elementary liberties. Your own old constitution, like those of your neighbours, contained pious statements which bore no relation to the old realities, though it must be said that they allowed some ingenious dissidents to make their case in the name of the letter of the law against the realities of power. This is why even pious texts are not entirely useless.

However, the key to giving basic rights the teeth which they need to bite, is the rule of law. In our conversation, I tried to impress upon you the primordial importance of this concept. In theory, it is not an easy concept to establish. What if the law itself is rotten? In the early weeks of his rule, Hitler pushed a number of laws through what was left of the last elected *Reichstag* under the Weimar Constitution, which reminds us that the rule of law is more than the rule of laws of any description. In fact, Hitler's Enabling Law established precisely the kind of monopoly which you are trying to demolish. In practice, the issue is not quite as difficult. The rule of law is not just about having legal texts to refer to; it is about the effective substance of these texts. This in turn can ultimately be guaranteed only by an independent judiciary which is seen to be incorruptible and fair, and which includes those who guard the constitution itself and its principles.

This too is a tall order. You referred to it when you asked me what should be done about the many lower-level judges who had administered communist 'laws' quite happily, and without any outward signs of disgust or dismay. Replacing those at the top without politicising the judiciary, and grooming a new generation to enter at the bottom, is probably the only realistic answer even if it obviously takes much longer than the six months which I have allotted for constitutional change. Beyond that, this is one of the moments at which one can do worse than turn to the *Federalist*, and notably to Hamilton's discussion of the judiciary.

Of course the judiciary has to be independent from the legislature and the executive. But as such this means little; as Hamilton notes, 'The judiciary is beyond comparison the weakest of the three departments of power . . . It may truly be said to have neither Force nor Will, but merely judgment; and must ultimately depend upon the aid of the executive arm even for the efficacy of its judgments.' So, what can be done? 'Permanency in office' and 'a fixed provision for their support' are obviously two things judges need.

The court system itself can help, with a well-designed balance between a Supreme Court and lower courts. There is the important issue of the role of juries. Then due process has to be established. I mention these points partly in order to impress on you the qualities of the constitution-building process of the United States, and partly to indicate that there are procedural means of giving the law clout. Others are more qualified than I am to pursue them in detail.

The rule of law is of course all-pervasive, at least so far as the rules of the democratic game are concerned. These require much thought themselves. Rather than write about federalism, electoral systems, party finance, two-chamber arrangements and the like, I want to reiterate one point of principle in this connection. No one can fail to understand that as you construct the constitution of liberty out of the ruins of the old monopoly of one party, your first concern is how to divide and dissipate power. Let there be as much democracy as possible! is the maxim on most constitution-builders' minds, and by democracy they mean not only the power of the people but above all the absence of power in the hands of the few, whoever they are. Thus proportional representation and referenda are piled upon decentralisation, administrative review and parliamentary prerogative. You want to know how to dismiss governments rather than how to make them strong. This is all very well, but it may add to your woes, especially in view of the vexing relation between politics and economics. In the valley of tears you want to make sure that government keeps its nerve and is not thrown off course by the kind-hearted desire to soothe people's pain, which bodes disaster in the medium term. The important point is to find a proper equilibrium of checks and balances on the one hand, and the ability of governments to govern on the other.

Let me just mention that in this respect too there is no patent solution. President Gorbachev was probably wrong to believe that he needed the extraordinary powers which some mistakenly associate with the American Presidency in order to do what needs to be done. Your own Prime Minister has relatively little power in purely constitutional terms, and yet he presided over one of the most drastic economic reforms of recent history. Formal power is no substitute for substantive policies. Even in formal terms, there are several methods of encouraging government initiative without paving the way for a new dictatorship. The British Prime Minister has unusual powers within a parliamentary democracy, which has to do with his or her effective control over the majority in Parliament and also with his or her residual right to dissolve Parliament and call elections. The West German Chancellor's more formal *Richtlinienkompetenz*, the constitutional entitlement to set guidelines of policy, is often made illusory by the requirements of coalition government, to say nothing of bureaucratic obstacles to its exercise. Most European democracies do not recognise a formal separation of powers; executive and legislature are usually closely linked. Their separation and built-in mix of co-operation and conflict is of course the main check on Presidential power in the United States. Perhaps the most relevant public debate about this issue is currently carried on in Italy, where a long period of five-party coalition government has made many people feel that nothing moves any more. This is what you want to avoid. Thus whatever specific pattern is chosen, it has to protect and enable at the same time: to protect the country from tyranny, and to enable its government to govern.

This then leads us back to the economic elements which belong in the constitution rather than the realm of normal politics. I have mentioned private property, contract and certain basic economic freedoms. Constitutional economists would like to go much further. Relations between the central bank and government, for example, raise an important question, and there is much to be said for an independent central bank. The key yet again is the breakup of all forms of monopoly. Anything that smacks of a state monopoly over economic processes has to be removed from the basic rules of the game. Here, more than in the field of political structures, the experience of others is relevant. When the Chinese leaders were still bent on reform, they realised this and had a separate minister for economic law who toured the democracies of the world; he must have amassed a great deal of useful material without being able to use it in China. In the Soviet Union, too, the relation between law and economics has been a major preoccupation. And of course there is East Germany, where one can watch the introduction of an entire set of new legal rules for economic behaviour in the form of the old rules of West Germany, though the film will have to be played in slow motion to make any sense to others.

So much for the hour of the (constitutional) lawyers. Next there is the hour of the politicians. After the constitution normal politics takes over. Even as I write this, I feel that my words may be misleading. I am not really talking about an organised sequence of events, with constitution-building first and economic policy next. In fact, both processes have to be set in motion at the same time. The difference – and the tension – lies in the fact that whereas constitutional politics encompasses the rules of both political and economic change, the process of normal politics splits the two and even sets them against each other. This is where the incompatible time scales of political and economic reform become relevant, and each threatens the other. Did I hear Lech Walesa say in a recent speech that perhaps democracy has to be suspended for a while in order to allow economic reforms to proceed? I have certainly heard those in Czechoslovakia who would like to slow down economic change in order to preserve democracy. Let me speculate a little on what would have to happen to make such contradictions bearable, and how it would have to be brought about, or rather, let me tell a story which encourages such speculation and – who knows? – even action.

Breaking the economic monopoly means of necessity the introduction of elements of the market. Whatever notions we use – prices, competition, incentives, even contract – they all involve a plurality of actors who are not co-ordinated by *Gosplan* or any other bureaucratic monster, but by less visible hands. Actually, some of the hands may be more visible than others; pure textbook capitalism is, as I have tried to show, neither a very likely nor a very desirable option; reality is never pure, and liberty is by definition multifarious and somewhat disorganised. Thus some kind of market economy follows from the constitutional changes required to build an open society. This, however, might well be a social market economy.

I can see you sit up: a 'third way' after all? No, it is nothing of the kind. Let me give you my version of the West German experience from which the term 'social market economy' derives. It is not a model, let alone a system, but it is an experience worth pondering on the road to freedom. It all began with the currency reform of 20 June 1948. Overnight the old *Reichsmark* lost its value, and the *Deutsche Mark* was introduced in the British, French and American occupation zones (thus incidentally setting in motion the division of Germany which ended forty-one years later with the breaching of the wall). The gist of this process was that a basic entitlement to real money was granted to everybody; it actually began with every citizen receiving 40 deutschmarks in cash, a kind of entry ticket for all to the new-found market. Over time, personal savings could be converted at the rate of 10:1, but to all intents and purposes this was a Zero Hour of socioeconomic life.

The technical measure of the currency reform had

been devised by the Allies and introduced with the help of the precursor of the West German Parliament, the Economic Council. It turned out to be equally critical, however, that in March 1948 this Council had appointed an Economic Director by the name of Ludwig Erhard. In the middle of the war, in 1943, Erhard, then a professor at the Nuremberg trade college, had written a private memorandum about the post-war economy, in which he assumed Germany's defeat and stated unambiguously that 'the goal to be aimed at remains in any case the free market economy based on genuine competition of achievement and guided by the intrinsic regulators of any economy.' In 1948 and for fifteen subsequent years, Erhard proceeded to practise what he had preached. He immediately freed most prices and all rationing. Helmut Schmidt has reminded us recently that some things took a little longer; rent control, for example, stayed in force for a few years, and full convertibility of the deutschmark was not achieved until the late 1950s. But the strategic decision to free prices was taken right away, and its consequences were dramatic. The black market collapsed and goods appeared in the shops; however, most people could not afford them, so they grumbled and worried, and the Social Democrats put a motion of no confidence to parliament. But Ludwig Erhard survived, by a majority of one, and stayed stubbornly on his course until things got better.

Despite his title of professor, Erhard was not a theorist. His theory came from another source, notably from his adviser Alfred Müller-Armack, who became his state secretary in 1952. Müller-Armack had invented the term, 'social market economy', *soziale Marktwirtschaft*. His 1949 paper, 'Proposals for the Implementation of the Social Market Economy', is almost the *Federalist Paper* for economic reform. It discusses the constitutional prerequisites of the market, the conditions of an effective transition, and the areas in which it is necessary to introduce social measures. The latter do not make a very impressive list. Employees must be treated humanely without restricting the responsibility of entrepreneurs. Competition must be regulated by certain rules. An anti-monopoly policy is needed. Only when he came to housing and social insurance did Müller-Armack show signs of going beyond the pure doctrine of the invisible hand.

It is therefore not surprising that Müller-Armack claimed that 'in the future we have to decide between two fundamentally different economic systems, namely the system of anti-market economic planning, and the system of a market economy based on free price formation, genuine competition of achievement and social justice.' The word justice apart, not much of this concept strikes one as particularly social. But then, Müller-Armack was the theorist and Erhard the practitioner. Erhard did not hesitate to intervene when it seemed indicated. He was certainly no Hayekian. His philippics against abuses of freedom and admonitions for a kind of moral market behaviour were laughed at by some at the time, but could not fail to have an effect, especially since he never hesitated to address the sinners directly and bluntly.

However, this is still only half the story. Erhard was a member of a government headed by the Catholic politician Konrad Adenauer. Actually, when Erhard, the liberal Protestant, was appointed, he was not even a member of the party which he was to lead fifteen years later, the Christian Democratic Union (CDU). In the early years of the Federal Republic, the CDU was strongly influenced by the Papal encyclicals on social reform, *Rerum Novarum* (1891) and *Quadragesimo Anno* (1931). It was also led by a man who, apart from his Catholicism, knew how to get and to keep power and therefore concluded an early compact with the trade unions, led by Hans Böckler. Add to that the indirect but strong influence of the occupation powers, and particularly the British trade unionist-become-Foreign Secretary Ernest Bevin, and you begin to understand how it came about that one and the same government preached Müller-Armack's system and introduced co-determination in the coal and steel industry, a highly participative 'constitution of the enterprise' for all and an elaborate and expensive scheme of old age pensions as well as health care, all of which made Germany one of the foremost welfare states of Europe.

There is obviously more to this story, more history, more politics, and more accident both in the sense of chance events and of costly mistakes. But the main point remains. Ludwig Erhard liked the term 'social market economy', which his mentor and adviser Alfred

Müller-Armack had whispered into his ear. But his own policy preferences hardly warranted the word 'social'. In the last analysis he believed that the market itself would resolve all social problems if only it was allowed to generate sufficient growth. The social element of the German economy entered through another door, the 'employees' wing' of the Christian Democratic Union, which contained in its programme Catholic reform thinking and trade union doctrine. The social market economy is in fact a hybrid, even a concoction of seemingly incompatible ingredients, but in the German case they turned out to produce a rather wholesome brew. Thus there is no 'system' which could be called 'social market economy'; there is only a reality which has come about under special, though not necessarily unique, circumstances.

The valley of tears in the case of the Federal Republic lasted four, if not five years. Indeed, it almost cost the CDU the first Federal elections a year and a quarter after the currency reform of 1948 and Erhard's early measures of liberalisation. Apart from votes of no confidence there were constant protests against what the Social Democrats called a policy for the rich which made the poor poorer. However, a number of factors helped Ludwig Erhard. One was the dismal condition of most Germans when he started. Things could only get better. Another was the post-war economic climate, influenced to no small extent by the American boom which had started at the beginning of the 1940s. A further factor was of course the Marshall Plan, the effect of which turned out to be particularly favourable in Germany. Without doubt, the blood, toil and tears of the trek through the valley were mitigated also by the social policies which accompanied economic recovery. In this way, a sufficient number of voters felt by the time of the second Federal elections in September 1953 that the bottom of the valley had been passed and things were improving. They helped increase support for Adenauer's party and, another four years later, led it to an overall majority in parliament.

There are many lessons from the German story. The most important one is that there is no such thing as a seamless economic policy. Even the favourite 'model' of most, the German social market economy, is in fact a hybrid of ideas and personalities. The open society wins. Then there is the role of the Marshall Plan, and of the conjuncture of the world economy. But as we wonder how it was done, one less obvious point strikes the eye. It has to do with a peculiar, rare, though not necessarily unique constellation of persons. This is a triangular constellation. At the top towers Adenauer, who had the stature and the standing to provide political cover for the others. Without him, Ludwig Erhard could not have pursued his determined course of liberalisation. When Ludwig Erhard himself became Chancellor in 1963, he signally failed to demonstrate similar stature and standing. However, under the protective umbrella of Adenauer's political clout and sense of purpose, and with the assistance of Müller-Armack, who produced both the necessary ideas and a plausible language to 'sell' them, Erhard put his name in the history books as the 'father of the social market economy'. By rights, he should share this epithet with the occupants of the third corner of the triangle who are almost forgotten today, notably Theodor Blank, the first Federal minister of social affairs, Hans Katzer, the early chairman of the 'Employees' Committees' of the CDU, and the leader of the German Trades Union Council, Hans Böckler.

You may think that I have strayed a long way from the post-communist world, but I assure you that in my mind I have not. My subject is still the relationship between political and economic reform, and the question of how to sustain the tensions between them and turn them to the benefit of the people. The conclusion is that it takes more than one political leader to achieve this feat. Somebody has to provide the protection of political power, somebody has to have the practical courage to take an economy from central planning to more open pastures, and somebody has to insist on certain social policies which are appropriate in their own right and also make the harsher side effects of the new-found market bearable. Mazowiecki, Balcerowicz and Jacek Kuron perhaps? I do not know. Nor is it likely that many countries will be blessed with the whole triad at the same time. But in terms of the normal politics of transition it is clearly highly desirable. The fact that President Gorbachev has not found such a constellation may well be one of the reasons why his *perestroika* is such a failure.

The formal process of constitutional reform takes

at least six months; a general sense that things are moving up as a result of economic reform is unlikely to spread before six years have passed; the third condition of the road to freedom is to provide the social foundations which transform the constitution and the economy from fair-weather into all-weather institutions which can withstand the storms generated within and without, and sixty years are barely enough to lay these foundations. We are today witnessing a great historical test of such an attempt, as the Federal Republic of Germany is challenged after forty years of steady development by German unification and a new role in Europe to prove the mettle of its democracy, prosperity and civil society. Civil society is the key. It pulls the divergent time scales and dimensions of political and economic reform together. It is the ground in which both have to be anchored in order not to be blown away. The hour of the lawyer and the hour of the politician mean little without the hour of the citizen.

Civil society is fashionable in East Central Europe. Timothy Garton Ash has described its 'central role in opposition thinking': 'There should be forms of association, national, regional, local, professional, which would be voluntary, authentic, democratic and, first and last, not controlled or manipulated by the Party or Party-state. People should be "civil": that is, polite, tolerant and above all, non-violent. Civil and civilian. The idea of citizenship had to be taken seriously.' Garton Ash surmises that 'ordinary men and women's rudimentary notion of what it meant to build a civil society might not satisfy the political theorist'. If it does not, one reason has to do with time horizons. The voluntary, authentic, democratic associations of the honeymoon of change can collapse and die as quickly as they have been brought to life. There were tears when the East German New Forum ended up with 2.9 per cent in the 1990 elections, and some Forum-type groups in the other countries have since joined the same route to oblivion. Your compatriot Adam Michnik, by temperament and circumstance always in a hurry, has described the first year of Solidarity's existence as 'the promise of a civil society'. I heard him say: 'When we realised that we were slaves, we knew that we had become citizens.' Moving words, but words about citizens at heart rather than in the real world. When T. H. Marshall wrote about citizenship in Britain, he allowed three centuries for the blossoming of the idea.

Building institutions, and a civil society at that, is a profoundly difficult notion. The godfather of this letter, Edmund Burke, liked the concept of civil society. But although he averred that 'civil society be made for the advantage of men' he only half believed the word 'made' in this statement. 'Society is indeed a contract,' he wrote, but the partnership created by this contract 'cannot be obtained in many generations, it becomes a partnership not only between those who are living, those who are dead, and those who are to be born.' It is also 'a clause in the great primaeval contract of eternal society'. Burke was fortunate, living as he did in England more than five hundred years after the Magna Carta. James Madison lived on more virgin territory. He had to invent institutions in order to create them. 'Justice is the end of government,' Madison wrote in the *Federalist*. 'It is the end of civil society.' This requires not just the separation of powers and decentralised government, but also more practical safeguards. Representation is one such safeguard; Madison recognised early that plebiscites and referenda can be tyrannical in effect. Size is a safeguard; minorities in small societies are more threatened than in large ones. But then he espoused an ingenious idea: 'Whilst all authority will be derived from and dependent on the society, the society itself will be broken into so many parts, interests and classes of citizens, that the rights of individuals or of the minority, will be in little danger from the interested combinations of the majority.' In other words, a multiplicity of groups and organisations and associations provides sufficient checks and balances against any usurpation of power.

Burke and Madison were not primarily worried about the state; in their time it had not yet acquired the Hegelian capital S which makes it one of the great threats to liberty in the twentieth century. Nowadays – for Adam Michnik, Janos Kis and many 'ordinary men and women' – civil society is about substantial sources of power outside the state, and more often than not, against the state. It means the creation of a tight network of autonomous institutions and organisations which has not one but a thousand centres and can therefore not easily be destroyed by a monopolist

in the guise of a government or a party. Civil society*
in a certain sense sustains itself. It does not seem to
need the state. One thinks of Italian society, Mafia
and all, though this codicil indicates the risk which a
civil society runs if there are not at the same time
certain rules and procedures binding on everyone.
This is why I prefer to think of civil society as providing
the anchorage for the constitution of liberty, including
its economic ingredients. Both are needed, civil society and the state, but they each have their own *raison
d'être* and their own autonomous reality.

Can one *build* a civil society in this sense? We must
try. Citizenship certainly can be built. The entitlements associated with membership of a society – a
national society until there is a world society – are a
matter of legislation and supporting policies. Civil,
political and social rights must become a part of the
fabric of the social and political community. The
creative chaos of organisations, associations and institutions is not as easily built, and should perhaps not
be the task of deliberate construction at all. Such
deliberateness is all too likely to produce a Brasilia
rather than a Rio de Janeiro, an artificial construct
which people yearn to escape for the nooks and cran-
nies of the real thing. Variety must be encouraged;
the task of deliberate action is one of enabling rather
than planning or even building. Small business must
be allowed and promoted. The media must be free
and pluralistic in outlook. Political parties must be
properly financed and independent of the state. (Arguably it is not such a good idea to anchor their existence

and internal structure in an article of the constitution.) Major institutions must be permitted to govern themselves even if their wherewithal depends in part on the government. This is true for the churches, the universities, the arts. Licensing processes for voluntary organisations must be reduced to a bare minimum. The law as well as levels and methods of taxation must encourage the establishment of foundations and other vehicles of philanthropy. A principle of subsidiarity should pervade the whole community by which the state only enters the scene when no one else can be persuaded to perform.

All this and much else is a tall order, and yet it is far from sufficient. If autonomy can be given, it can also be taken away. If organisations depend on funding, and public funding at that, they are always at risk. The secret of the United States of America is of course that civil society was there first, and the state came later, by the grace of civil society, as it were. The whole point of *The Federalist Papers* is after all to give reasons why there should be a federal government at all and under which conditions it is bearable. Similarly in England, absolutist rulers never prevailed over the barons and other sources of local power to the extent to which they did on the Continent. Switzerland is even today more a civil society, if a highly organised one, than a state. On the other hand, countries which had to create civil societies after the event were and are in trouble. Here, citizens have to borrow power from those whom they want to keep in check.

This is notably true in the post-communist world.

'We are the people' is a nice slogan but as a constitutional maxim it is a mirror image of the total state which has just been dislodged. If the monopoly of the Party is replaced merely by the victory of the masses, all will be lost before long, for the masses have no structure and no permanence. Once again, you are lucky in Poland, as Adam Michnik noticed almost instinctively, and one must hope that the relative retreat of the Church and the probable fragmentation of Solidarity will not destroy the principles on which your national freedom is based. The key question is how to fill the gap between the state and the people – sometimes, as in Romania, one of frightening dimensions – with activities which by their autonomy create social sources of power. Before this is achieved, the constitution of liberty and even the market economy, social or otherwise, will remain suspended in mid-air.

What is needed apart from deliberate efforts and an enabling climate of public affairs, is a frame of mind. Garton Ash was right to throw in the words 'civil and civilian' at this point. A civil society is civil, even civilised, and this requires men and women who respect others, but more important still, who are able and willing to go and do things themselves by encouraging others and creating the necessary vehicles of action, confident men and women who are not frightened and have no reason for fear, citizens. I do not particularly like notions like 'active citizenship', which seem to place all the emphasis on the obligations associated with membership of society. There are such obligations to be sure, like complying with the law, or paying taxes; but they should be kept at a minimum and should not include, for example, compulsory voting. The right not to vote is as important as the right not to work. Moreover, obligations must be seen in their own right, and not turned into prerequisites of the entitlements of citizenship. Citizenship rights are in principle unconditional. 'No representation without taxation' – a genuine 'poll tax' – would be a perversion of citizenship, as would a form of 'workfare' which makes elementary social benefits dependent on people working, and thereby introduces forced labour through the back door. But when all is said and done, it remains the case that citizenship is not just a passive status. It is an opportunity, a chance to live an active and full life of participation in the political process, the labour market, society. To do so effectively, certain civic virtues are indispensable, including civility, but also self-reliance. This is the facet of civil society which cannot be built at all; it has to grow, and it will not grow in a season or even a parliamentary period. Sixty years may be an overly discouraging time horizon for civil society to become real; in any case conditions differ from country to country and from society to society; but a generation is needed at least, and perhaps in this respect too we have to wait for the 'two-turnover test' – though of generations rather than elections.

You will not have failed to notice that as I went on with this route finder for the road to freedom (it is hardly a theory), the mood of my argument has become gloomier. The hour of the lawyer is euphoric and filled with visible progress; the hour of the politician is tense at times but exhilarating at others; the hour of the citizen drags on through numerous ups and downs, and its success can never really be measured. Let us face it, therefore: the entire route which I have tried to trace is full of pitfalls and risks. To repeat, freedom does not just happen. It has to be created; it has to be defended at every point of the process; the attempt can fail. Some sources of failure are obvious, and also hard to avoid. The right leaders may not come up, or those who lead may become faint-hearted. Not every country is lucky enough to have an Adenauer and an Erhard, or a Juan Carlos and an Adolfo Suarez, later a Felipe Gonzalez at the same time. Still, your Polish leadership sets a good example, and there is Vaclav Havel in Prague. To some extent, great historical opportunities seem to find their masters.

More serious causes of failure arise from the project of freedom itself. In some post-communist countries it looks as if the collapse of the centre has reached proportions which make it difficult for anyone or any group to hold things together sufficiently to bring about effective reform. East Germany seemed at one point close to this condition, but is now saved by a unification which extends the legal and political structures of the Federal Republic to what used to be the GDR. Romania may be another example. Even where this is not the case, mistakes can be made in the hour of the lawyers, at the constitutional level. It is hard to resist the temptation to let feelings of revenge get the better of the knowledge that the rule of law must prevail. The Italian Communist (or whatever he is called now) Sergio Segre was quite right when he attacked East Germans for arresting their former leader Erich Honecker: 'Will you never learn from history? Is the era of the trials of the 1930s and 1950s going to start all over again? These are politically beaten people; leave them in peace in their defeat; do not begin the old stories again. Otherwise one will never start anything new.' Latin America shows the consequences. Arguably the greatest weakness of the old states of Latin America is that most of them have never managed to give the rule of law reality in the institutions of society and the hearts and minds of the people. Their leaders and many of their people have either condoned the crimes of previous regimes or taken revenge. Condoning them destroys public morality, and revenge breeds violence. Neither is conducive to the establishment of liberty. The vicious circle must be broken.

Other constitutional mistakes are in the cards. The balance of democracy and leadership which I have advocated may not be reached at the first try. In fact, many of the initial rules may look unworkable or undesirable after they have been tried. Again one thinks of Latin America, though Germany provides another example. The history of some countries has become a cemetery of constitutions. In the end no one trusts their paper promises any more than paper money when inflation runs at 2,000 per cent. Among other strengths of the American Constitution there is this: that it is short and lives through its brief amendments and the interpretations of the Supreme Court. Admittedly, the Constitution also got it right in most respects. Britain, as you know, has no written constitution at all, which may have been all right in the days of Edmund Burke but is certainly a deficiency today when it comes to the rule of law. I am not sure what to conclude from such observations nor will you be, I suppose, except that it is probably better for the initial constitution to err on the short side than to be too elaborate.

Then there is the dilemma of political and economic reform, the dangerous trip through the valley of tears. Whoever has embarked on it must not give up or turn back, and embarking on it is as indispensable as constitutional reform. But one does not have to go unprovisioned and unprotected. There is no need to make life harder than it is in any case; apart from emergency rations and a bit of entertainment at night, one can think of various forms of relief. The most important point to remember is that there is no such thing as a seamless economic policy, important though it is to have one reformer on board who has a clear vision and the nerve to pursue it against many odds.

Failure looms large on the horizon as we seek the road to freedom. *El desencanto* is almost inevitable, and worse states of mind and of affairs than mere disenchantment are certainly conceivable. What would such failure mean? Where would it lead countries which have freed themselves of the monopoly of one-party *nomenklatura* socialism? Not, I am sure, back to the old regime. At least in its negative aspect, the revolution in Europe is an irreversible process.

The reason for this confident assertion is simple; one could probably spell it out by analysing the predicament of Gorbachev's 'conservative enemy' Yegor Ligachev. There are undoubtedly those members of the former *nomenklatura* who think back wistfully to the cosy world of Brezhnev, *dacha*, armoured limousine, 99 per cent 'vote' and all. In due course, they will probably tell us that the old regime was not as bad as we now think, and in many ways preferable to the shambles which the revolution has left behind. But even if by some fluke they – say, Ligachev – were to gain supreme power, they could not do much more than tell all and sundry, 'I told you so.' The old regime was, in its last phase at least, a sham. It collapsed at fairly slight provocation. There was not only no popular support for it – which after the elections of 1990 is evident for all – but even without such support, state, party and economy had lost the ability to function. As the example shows, this world of pretence can happen, but it cannot be created, let alone recreated. In this sense, communism is gone, never to return.

But as I have emphasised throughout, there are many alternatives of which the road to freedom is only one. It is quite conceivable that a Ligachev may preside over a messy mixture of the half-hearted return to some form of central planning, a military which tries to maintain law and order and preserve the Union, and sullen acceptance of continued misery by the people. In East Central Europe, many unhappy combinations are thinkable. Quickly changing governments and even regimes which leave few traces other than a near-total disenchantment are as possible as new political monopolies coupled with a degree of market conditions for the economy, and as prolonged states of confusion and disorientation.

The greatest risk is probably of another kind altogether. I hesitate to use the word, but it is hard to banish from one's thoughts: fascism. By that I mean the combination of a nostalgic ideology of community which draws harsh boundaries between those who belong and those who do not, with a new political monopoly of a man or a 'movement' and a strong emphasis on organisation and mobilisation rather than freedom of choice. The rule of law would be suspended; dissidents and deviants would be incarcerated; minorities would be singled out for popular wrath and official discrimination. Fascism in this sense need not be as horrific as German National Socialism; systematic genocide is not a necessary consequence of its rule, though it is always likely. It is in any case a tyranny which has its origin on what we have got used to calling the right, because it is allied with the military, the other forces of 'law and order', it appeals to reactionary sentiments and it dreams of the purity of a bygone age rather than Utopian visions of a better future. Such fascism can have many names, Mussolini and Franco, Peron and Pinochet.

This risk comes to mind not just because of the prospect of the valley of tears, the seemingly irremediable collapse of the centre of authority, or even the possibility of a profound disenchantment on the part of a majority with the promises of democracy. The rise of anti-Semitism and of a nationalism which has little to do with the nation-state and much with ethnic homogeneity and resentment of those who are different, are more important factors. But above all, certain social processes are emerging in at least some countries of East Central Europe (including, quite emphatically, the former German Democratic Republic) which bear an uncanny resemblance to the syndrome which gave birth to fascism in the 1920s.

We still encounter in the literature competing explanations of Nazism and the milder versions of fascism. Some cling to the belief that fascism is an outgrowth of mass society in which all structures of class and of party have been dismantled. Others, notably in your part of the world, have abandoned many tenets of Marxism-Leninism but not the thesis that fascism is somehow the sinister climax of capitalism. (The compelling conclusion, therefore, is that capitalism must be avoided at all costs.) Both explanations founder on the simple fact that the one society of the world which was most nearly a mass society as well as an incarnation of capitalism, that of the United States of America, has also proved entirely immune to the temptation. It is true that Henry Ford published the alleged 'Protocols of the Elders of Zion' in his *Dearborn Independent* in the early 1920s just before they were revealed to have been forged by the Tsarist secret police; but the great capitalist did not persuade the masses of Detroit and perhaps remained unconvinced himself of the Jewish conspiracy for world domination. After the great depression, America chose Roosevelt and reform instead of Hitler and terror and war. And that other firmly capitalist country, Britain, muddled through the difficult 1920s and 1930s with democracy and the rule of law unimpaired.

The soil in which fascism thrives is made of different earth. Its prime characteristic is the sudden impact of the forces of the modern industrial world on a society which is unprepared because it has retained many of the characteristics of an older, status-ridden, authoritarian age. The two simply do not match. As a result, important groups find themselves dislocated and disoriented. They are stuck halfway between old and new. They hate capitalism as much as socialism, the newly rich as much as the newly poor. They are farmers and shopkeepers but also members of the new middle class by status and education, civil servants, white-collar workers, even engineers. In this condition, a political movement which promises to destroy the present and return the past has great appeal, and few recognise in time that there can be no return to old pastures. In effect, fascism is above all a destructive force, and soon crude power takes the place of all ideologies. But once people notice the trap into which they have walked and the *Bildungsbürger* begin to regret the early professions of loyalty which helped to stabilise a regime of terror, it is too late.

It would be quite wrong to apply this analysis to the post-communist world without important qualifications. For one thing, if communism is modernisation for latecomers, it is still a form of modernisation. For another thing, there are great differences between countries. Most have actually been through the purgatory, if not the hell of fascism, and I firmly believe that in this respect as in others we do not step into the same rivers twice. But the extent to which outdated social structures have been preserved in the communist countries is striking. These may not be preindustrial authoritarian structures; they resemble more our own conditions of Europe in the immediate post-war years. Philip Roth goes back even further. 'There is still a pre-World War II varnish on the societies that, since the forties, have been under Soviet domination. The countries of the satellite world have been caught in a time warp.' They awake with a shock, a personal shock to begin with. Roth quotes Helena Klimova to the effect that 'neurotics are getting worse' because all structure is gone and 'they are suddenly in a world of choices'. Karl Heinz Bohrer has described the curious *Doppelgängereffekt* of East Germany on West Germans: West Germans are irritated because 'they see their history, their past come back to them'. What do East Germans see? There is certainly a sense of dislocation. Personal shocks are translated into social shocks. Dream and reality fall apart, unless someone comes along with the false promise to put them together again.

As you know, I was unimpressed and even upset about your emphatic defence of cheap books and the cultural virtues of life in the old regime. You really cannot have it both ways, and if you try, the price will be high. You will have to let the huge wave of modernity, market, glitter and all, roll over you and make sure that you come up again once it has passed, otherwise the risk of a fascist backlash will be even greater. I hate to think of the combination of military leaders, economic planners and racist ideologists which might be brought to power by dislocated and disenchanted groups. Guard against the beginnings! Fundamentalists are waiting around many corners to collect their contributions from those who have lost their nerve on the road to freedom.

Such consequences of failure are bad enough. But I have not even mentioned one set of issues which belongs squarely in my argument and has to do with the outside world. So far, I have for the most part argued as if every post-communist society could go its own way undisturbed by others like it or by powers outside its orbit. Your anxious questions about Germany and Europe made it clear that you are not as sanguine in this respect. Nor am I. A Soviet invasion is not the only danger to the new democracies; it may well be the least threatening prospect, at least for the independent countries of East Central Europe. (The Soviet republics striving for independence unfortunately evoke the spectre of Tiananmen Square.) We must guard against paranoia. The rest of Europe, and the superpowers beyond, are as much an opportunity as a threat. But they raise questions both about the conditions of success and the consequences of failure on the road to freedom.

Mostly about Germany and the New Architecture of Europe

The gist of my argument in this letter is that the countries which have shed really existing socialism have not embraced another system such as capitalism instead; they have chosen the open society in which there are a hundred different ways forward to freedom, and a handful on offer at any one time. By the same token, these countries have not abandoned the East in order to join the West; they want to join Europe. Timothy Garton Ash detected this desire three years before the revolution of 1989 in his essay 'Does Central Europe Exist?': 'We are to understand that what was *truly* Central European was always Western, rational, humanistic, democratic, sceptical, and tolerant. The rest was East European, Russian, or possibly German.' He has made the point again after the event (and this time without the 'Central'): 'Travelling to and fro between the two halves of the divided continent, I have sometimes thought that the real divide is between those (in the West) who have Europe and those (in the East) who believe in it. And everywhere, in all the lands, the phrase people use to sum up what is happening is "the return to Europe".'

The first question which needs to be raised before we go any further is: Where is Europe? Or rather, Where is it not? Clearly, we are not talking about the grandiose design of a Europe stretching eastward from San Francisco to Vladivostok. There were good reasons why the Conference on Security and

Co-operation in Europe (CSCE) included Canada and the United States as well as the Soviet Union, but it was not intended to be a definition of Europe; Europe was, as it were, its object and not its subject. However European the United States, Canada (as well as Australia and New Zealand) may have been, they are not today a part of Europe. More serious issues arise nearer home. Some would like to define their Europe as extending from Brest on the French Atlantic coast to Brest on the Polish-Soviet border, thereby excluding not only the Soviet Union but Britain and Ireland as well. This is most unfair to the Irish, who have proved loyal and active Europeans in the European Community if not before. It is also deeply wrong for Britain. Whatever special relationships the United Kingdom may cherish with the United States of America and the Commonwealth, its destiny lies firmly in Europe. As former British Defence Minister Michael Heseltine put it, 'The tide of history has carried us close to Europe's shore. We should accept that destiny; the wind will never be more favourable.'

The more difficult question is that of the place of the Soviet Union but it also deserves an unambiguous answer. I have already shown my cards and said that so far as I am concerned, Europe ends at the Soviet border, wherever that may be. If Lithuania, Latvia and Estonia manage to establish their claim that they do not belong to the Soviet Union, then they are a part of Europe (though Azerbaijan would not be even if it attained independence), but otherwise Europe is almost co-extensive with the zone of Central European Time (for the sake of which Britain may soon abandon its cherished Greenwich Mean Time). In arguing this, I find myself in interesting company. The foreign-policy spokesman of the former Italian Communist Party, Giorgio Napoletano, told me that when he visited President Gorbachev with his then chairman Alessandro Natta, they opened the conversation by informing the inventor of the term that so far as they were concerned there was no 'common house' for both Italy and the Soviet Union; the Italians' common European home was that of the European Community plus the East Central European states. Willy Brandt, when challenged on the issue and asked whether he includes the Soviet Union in Europe, replied: 'No. The European house is one of those things. I do not believe that Vladivostok will in future belong to it.' The Soviet Union 'certainly has a strong European component and not just a good bit of European culture,' he went on, but relations with it are 'not the same problem as relations between Western Europe, Central Europe and the countries which in recent years have been called in a slightly overgeneralising fashion, Eastern Europe.'

Poor Vladivostok, which may in fact be more European than Yerevan or Baku! But the instinct of the two – socialist – leaders is relevant. Something is different about relations, say, between France and Poland, and between France and the Soviet Union; it also makes a difference whether Spain is asked to share a home with Hungary or with the Soviet Union, not to mention the feelings of East Central Europeans about their big neighbour. If I were to spell out the difference, three points would come to mind. One is that there is something suspicious about yesterday's hegemonic power wishing to set up house with those whom it occupied and held under its tutelage for so long; it is probably better to keep the grizzly bear outside. The second reason is that the Soviet Union, with all its European history, is a vast developing country which has a much longer way to go than others in its European orbit before it becomes a full part of the modern world. The third and most important point is that Europe is not just a geographical or even cultural concept, but one of acute political significance. This arises at least in part from the fact that small and medium-sized countries try to determine their destiny together. A superpower has no place in their midst, even if it is not an economic and perhaps no longer a political giant. The capacity to kill the whole of mankind several times over puts the Soviet Union in different company from Germany, Italy and Spain, Poland, Czechoslovakia and Hungary, and even the nuclear powers Britain and France.

If there is a common European house or home to aim for, it is therefore not Gorbachev's but one to the West of his and his successors' crumbling empire. Before I go on to your specific questions about Germany and Europe, another myth has to be exploded. For you and the people of Czechoslovakia, Hungary, Yugoslavia, Romania and perhaps even Bulgaria to speak of a 'return to Europe' rather than, say, the defection to the West is fine as long as Europe is not turned into a reified ideology. Europe is not a third way between East and West. It is not just one way at all. Hans Magnus Enzensberger has caught the charm and the uniqueness of this part of the world in his sketches in *Europe, Europe!* He looked at the periphery – Ireland, Portugal, Sweden, Hungary – and told stories of ordinary people and their lives. They may have something in common, if only that they are clearly not the lives of Koreans or Kenyans or even Colombians or Californians, but beyond such negatives it is the extraordinary cultural differences on this small peninsula appended to the vast continent of Asia which make Europe special. Europe will forever be a patchwork quilt of languages and of cultures of everyday life, politics and economics. For the countries which have at last escaped *nomenklatura* socialism, the return to Europe means therefore, like the open society, above all the chance to be themselves and not conform to an imposed hegemonic model.

This is a massive and consequential change. It ends over four decades which began in 1946 when George Kennan sent his 'long telegram' from Moscow about the limits of the Soviet interest in a common order for the world, and Winston Churchill made his 'Iron Curtain' speech in Fulton, Missouri. They were the decades of the Cold War. Perhaps the changes following from the revolution in Europe also make us (in President Mitterrand's words) *sortir de Yalta*, move away from Yalta and Potsdam, where Europe's post-war borders were set, though that is still an open question. They certainly put an end to the Brezhnevian monstrosity of the Helsinki Agreement to leave everything in Europe exactly as it was with mutual guarantees of the status quo and the fatuous prospect of replacing the Cold War by an equally Cold Peace. Fortunately, the Final Act did not quite succeed in this objective, but it is hard to see how it – or even the much-quoted 'CSCE process' – can help in designing the architecture of a new Europe of change and of liberty.

Change of course is not just desirable even when things are badly in need of it. It is also threatening. Old menaces had been contained by an unsatisfactory though familiar status quo, but as the status quo crumbles, they rise from the debris along with some new worries. One of the worries is Germany. It is amazing how quickly the German bogey has come to occupy the place of everybody's favourite enemy which was so long the exclusive property of the Soviet Union. Of André Fontaine's three 'reunifications', that of language is unreservedly welcome, that of Europe a pleasing if somewhat distant prospect, but that of Germany a threat for many. You put your finger on it: are we not going to see a balkanised Europe dominated by the one power which is uniting rather than disintegrating?

You will appreciate that this is a subject of special poignancy for a correspondent whose life has been marked by the push and pull of obligation to his country of birth, Germany, and temptation by his country of choice, Britain. When I decided (on two occasions) to accept invitations to live in Britain and throw in my lot with the world of Locke and Burke and Mill and of course Popper (or rather with the lesser mortals who dominate public discourse on the blessed if not altogether perfect island today), this had a great deal to do with my feelings about Germany. Thus I am anything but dispassionate in the matter. It upsets me when the bumbling West German Chancellor Helmut Kohl – whose sense of power is better developed than the power of his sensitivity – sacrifices your evident need to have secure borders for the sake of a few uncertain votes in the backwoods of Bavaria. When it comes to Germany, I am torn between hopes and fears, as I suppose many of us are all over Europe.

On the side of hope we must note above all the remarkable success of democracy in West Germany. I remember you asking for guarantees for the Polish borders, and looking to treaties signed by all parties and endorsed by the Allies. These may well be necessary; but ultimately there is only one guarantee, and that is a country which has overcome its historical neuroses by finding a mould which makes it unnecessary for its citizens to compensate for their dissatisfactions at home by creating havoc abroad. A reliable German democracy in the sense of both the constitution of liberty and civil society is a safer bet for you and for others than any piece of paper can ever be, however distinguished the signatures on it.

Let me go a step further. If we do not believe that German democracy is stable after forty years of proof – including the two-turnover test as it happens – how can we even begin to embark on the road to freedom in the post-communist world? Surely somewhere behind your efforts there lies the hope that given time the open society can become real and firmly anchored in Poland, Czechoslovakia, Hungary and elsewhere. If you believe that for yourselves, you must also believe it for others, and Germany is the prime candidate for such confidence after all those years.

I confess that in the 1950s I was far from happy about the way things were going in the Federal Republic. In fact, I talked rather like you do about contemporary Polish conditions, and like leading German intellectuals about the current process of unification. I was a social democrat then, and social democracy was still in opposition. A decade later I had come to realise that the reasons for my disquiet were merely the seedy side of remarkable progress. Adenauer was not (just) a clever old fox who pursued his Weimar dreams of a Rhine Republic irrespective of opposition, and Erhard not (just) insensitive to the poor and disadvantaged, but between them the two were creating the conditions for putting the ship of state on a steady course by joining it to the European fleet, and making sure that there was no shortage of provisions. When I wrote my book *Society and Democracy in Germany* in the mid 1960s, I had many critical things to say – after all, the country had not even passed its first turnover test – but I also argued that more had changed than just the political and economic surface of German society. A useful constitution, the Basic Law of 1949, had become living reality in the political conflicts between parties which had shed many of the antics and a lot of the sentiments of their Weimar predecessors, and underneath the new political climate, society had changed profoundly. 'Thanks' to the unintended side effects of Hitler's rule, Germany had at last joined the modern world, and was coming to terms with the fact that in the open society, one has to live with conflict and turn it to creative use rather than try to sweep it under the carpet and seek a false harmony which more often than not means tyranny.

There is no compelling reason why these gains should be in jeopardy as a result of the process of unification. It is true that people in the former GDR have not had forty years of exposure to the democratic way of life. Watching West German television is no substitute for living in a civil society. You were quite right to point out that at the border of Poland and East Germany, chauvinist incidents abound. The potential of the extreme right in the Eastern *Länder* of the new Germany is likely to be significantly greater than in the old Federal Republic. Nowhere is the personal and the social shock of the impact of the consumer society on the slow-motion world of declining *nomenklatura* socialism more extreme than in Eastern Germany where it was instant and total. Thus there is undoubtedly something like a fascist potential.

But there is also a deep desire to live like the cousins in the West and of course it will actually be satisfied. The desire may be superficial and purely materialistic at first, but other features of a Western lifestyle are bound to follow. All this might have been easier if there had been more impressive political leaders, especially in the old Federal Republic; but it must be noted that none of the leaders in sight shows the slightest doubt in the values of the constitution of liberty, civil society, and European co-operation. The most likely course is therefore a replay of some of the experiences of the 1950s, including their political majorities, and at the end of the day a larger, but essentially familiar Federal Republic of Germany.

But alas! hopes and fears are so close. Talk to German intellectuals about a replay of the 1950s and you will see their hackles rise. This is precisely what they do not want, and it is one of the reasons why yet again the intelligentsia is at odds with history. Some think that this does not matter. Ludwig Erhard thought so, and probably Chancellor Kohl does, too. The view was mistaken in the 1950s, as its proponents discovered to their cost in the turbulent 1960s; it is mistaken today for an even more serious reason. This has to do with the vexing issue of the German nation, which is one of two reasons for apprehension about the new Germany, the other having to do with Europe.

Helmut Kohl likes few words as much as 'father-land'. When he speaks of the *Vaterland*, the deep, almost Wagnerian sound resonates through his not inconsiderable frame, so that often, and characteristi-cally, he tries to sweeten it a little by adding an adjective like *wunderschön*. 'Our wondrously beautiful fatherland' is what he is about. What exactly it means is not so easy to tell; but certainly the language annoys more critical minds. So they go to the other extreme.

Günter Grass, for example, felt prompted to write a piece in which he proudly described himself as a *vaterlandslose Geselle*, a fellow without a fatherland, which is how the right used to describe Social Democrats before the First World War, and some even later. 'I not only fear a Germany simplified into one state from two states,' Grass wrote, 'but I reject the united state and would be relieved if – whether by German insight or the objections of neighbours – it did not come about.' Pressed to substantiate his fears, Grass keeps coming back to one word, Auschwitz. 'Whoever thinks about Germany at present and seeks answers to the German question, must think of Auschwitz as well.'

I agree. But is it not too simple to imply an almost causal connection between a united Germany and Auschwitz? Is Grass not pushing responsibility away, to Bismarck, to mere facts of geopolitics, rather than placing it where it belongs, in the 'politics of cultural despair' perhaps, and the hundred inhumanities of everyday life? My friend Fritz Stern has contributed as much as anyone to our understanding of the 'temptations of totalitarianism', but for once I must disagree with him. When he addressed the West German *Bundestag* in 1988 on the occasion of the anniversary of 17 June 1953 when East Berlin workers rose against the communist regime, Stern said, 'The undivided Germany has brought untold misery for other peoples and for itself.' He did not mean Auschwitz, but the 'demons of hegemonic power', the two world wars. Even so, not being divided was hardly the prime reason, much less does it follow that unification means a return of the demons.

Even without Auschwitz, and the wars, there is enough cause for apprehension. The fact that many leading intellectuals cannot come to terms with reality is one of them. For Günter Grass is by no means alone. There is, to be sure, another side which has its own blind spots. Karl Heinz Bohrer is concerned about the parochialism of the Republic of Bonn and sees moral as well as almost aesthetic gains in unification. Martin Walser not only wants to be able to go to the theatre in Leipzig and Dresden without having to think about the German question, but regards nations as more-than-political, almost 'geological' powers. Brigitte Seebacher-Brandt refers to the 'imponderables of the soul of the people' which need to be taken into account. Ulrich Greiner, the cultural editor of *Die Zeit*, takes them all to task and muses: 'What actually speaks for German unity?' Two days before the East German elections of 18 March he asserted that 'the burden of proof rests with those who are singing the song of the German nation.' Does it really? I am almost tempted to invoke our old friend again, History with a capital H, but the voters of East Germany have relieved me of the need.

The core of the problem is that German intellectuals have not come to terms with the concept of nation. It was of course difficult to do so. The 'belated nation' (in Helmuth Plessner's phrase) remained precarious precisely because it was never clearly defined. But was there a need to add intellectual imprecision to geographic indefinition? Greiner quotes Max Weber, who shared the German problem with nationhood. For Weber, nation means 'first of all undoubtedly: that certain groups of people can be expected to show a specific sense of solidarity towards others; thus it belongs to the sphere of values.' Does it really? And 'undoubtedly'? I have more than just doubts, much as both a sense of solidarity and Solidarity have helped your own tragic nation on its remarkable path. The problem with German intellectuals is that most of them have always tried to make the case for – and against – the nation either with misplaced (economic) concreteness or with equally misplaced (cultural) vagueness, and in the process the real strength of nationhood slipped through their fingers.

One man who has not made either of these mistakes, and is nevertheless a sceptic with respect to German unity, is Jürgen Habermas. In a string of articles written since the peaceful revolution in East Germany he has developed his theme of 'constitutional patriotism'. He reserves his wrath for what he calls 'Deutschmark nationalism': 'One single unit of account for all subjects. German interests are weighed and pushed through by German *marks*.' In this respect, Timothy Garton Ash is more subtle when he points to the package of which the currency is merely the symbol; what the East Germans want is 'first the DM of course, but not just the DM, also the free press, the rule of law, local self-government, and federal democracy'. But Habermas knows that this package is burdened with history and always liable to fall apart.

A German state cannot be founded on 'prepolitical facts' of culture and national history; it has got to be a mere 'nation of citizens', and in that sense a 'non-nationalist nation'. Many had hoped (so Habermas argues) that this had become real in the Federal Republic, but the process of unification casts doubt on such hopes. We are reminded of the fact that contrary to 'the classic nation-states of the West', a sense of nationhood and a 'republican mentality' have not complemented each other in Germany since 1848. It is true, Habermas notes, that 'liberal institutions' have come to be broadly accepted in the Federal Republic after forty years: 'Even without the roots of a republican mentality, we have grown *accustomed* to the traditions of liberty.' The emphasis is by Habermas; he wants to say that it is not enough simply to grow accustomed to institutions. Is he dreaming of Burke's 'great primaeval contract of eternal society'? Certainly he hopes that the constitution of a new, unified Germany will be thoroughly debated and then put to the people so that the decision of the majority becomes a conscious act around which the republican mentality of future generations can be crystallised.

One may disagree with this prescription, and put more emphasis on people getting accustomed to traditions, but Habermas's argument tackles the critical questions. The point which is so often and so dangerously missed by Germans, be they intellectuals, politicians, or ordinary citizens, is that the nation-state is about the rule of law, and the constitution. It has to do with building, maintaining and developing institutions before the gross national product is totted up and the vapours of national sentiment rise. German unity is a unique opportunity to prove the point. Or is Habermas right after all? Do we have to talk already about an opportunity missed? Have the fatherland and the deutschmark been victorious, with the constitution coming a poor third, and institution-building very low on the agenda? In one sense, the map for the road to freedom which I sketched in response to your questions and those of the post-communist world, is a precept for the new Germany too. The country's intellectuals have not helped to make the point. They have been nebulous and negative instead of precise and constructive. This is why there is cause for worrying about the unified Germany which is awakening under our eyes.

It is one of the reasons for apprehension here. The other is equally serious, and links the failure to define the nation with false hopes in the new Europe. Both may not be peculiar to Germany – in any case, any German threat is a threat to its neighbours, and to the whole of Europe – but they are linked to the debate about German unity. Peter Glotz, the most articulate social democratic intellectual around, and a practising politician to boot, has tried to design a 'concept of the new Europe for the slowly and painfully emerging European Left'. He sees two threats to the incipient democratisation of Eastern Europe. One is 'the dawn of a new nationalism in Europe', notably as a result of what you called the process of 'balkanisation'; the other is the rise of populist forces of the right which try to resist European integration. Against them, Glotz holds the familiar thesis that 'at the end of the twentieth century the nation-state is economically, ecologically, militarily and culturally out of date'. We must move both down to the 'tribes', to regional autonomy, and up to 'supranational structures'. For Germany, this means that its development must not be primarily national; it must be absorbed into a wider process of European integration. Glotz is one of many who had to eat their words because they were overtaken by events as they rushed along the extraordinary months of 1989 and 1990. (Who knows? this may well happen to me with some of the things which I write in this letter.) He wrote in late 1989 that he would be happy to accept a decision by the citizens of the GDR to keep two German states alive for good, though he would hope that such a GDR would have a close association with the European Community. In any case, a 'social-democratic programme for Europe' aims at 'a pan-European federal state – with maximal guarantees for ethnic groups and minority rights.'

Alas! once again, as so often with German authors and politicians, one has to conclude that laudable sentiments are combined with muddled thinking and amazing ignorance of the facts of Europe. Leaving the reality of German unity on one side, there are, first of all, no signs of the European process of co-operation making the nation-state superfluous so far as its critical tasks are concerned. It is telling that in his list of outdated functions – economic, ecological, military, cultural – Glotz does not mention the law, or citizenship with its civil, political and social ingredients. Raymond Aron said many years ago that 'there are no such animals as "European citizens"': 'The Jews of my generation cannot forget how fragile these human rights become when they no longer correspond with citizenship rights.' Aron was of course aware of successive attempts to create a new, supranational citizenship in Europe. The first of these was the Council of Europe, founded in 1949, which now has twenty-two members. It is above all the guardian of the European Convention of Human Rights, which most though not all member states have read into their national law. The Council of Europe has a record of protecting democracy; when the Colonels took over in 1969, Greece had to give up membership. It might help the establishment of the rule of law if the new democracies of East Central Europe became members, and several have applied already. However, the Council of Europe is an intergovernmental rather than a supranational organisation. By contrast, the European Community (EC) is a strict 'community of law'. Resulting from a merger of three Communities in 1967 – the European Coal and Steel Community of 1951, the European Economic Community and the European Atomic Community of 1957 – it can take decisions which are binding on members, and are protected by the European Court, in those areas which are covered by the treaties. They are however mostly economic, and do not constitute a European citizenship. The much looser organisations of West European Union (WEU), based on co-operation in the defence field between

Europe's NATO members, and the European Free Trade Association (EFTA) which combines the mostly neutral democracies of Western Europe (Austria, Switzerland, Finland, Sweden, Norway, Iceland) which are not members of the EC, are even less designed to constitute a common citizenship.

Thus in today's Europe, the nation-state is to all intents and purposes still the repository of basic rights of citizenship, and West Germans should be proud of the fact that they can extend the benefits of this status to 16 million East Germans. Glotz's – and many other Germans' – notion of Europe is in fact too vague to be truly attractive. More than that, it is too vague to be credible. This is where the second major reason for concern about German developments enters the scene. It is all very well to talk about a Europe which combines regional autonomy with supranational institutions – but where are the signs of either of these, let alone their combination, happening? Worse still, many Germans use language like 'German unification must remain firmly embedded in the process of European integration' – but do they know what they are saying? And are they acting as if they believe it?

This is a sensitive and difficult issue. As you know, I have had occasion to watch Germany's attitude to the European Community at close quarters. As an EC Commissioner in Brussels in the early 1970s, I listened attentively to the arguments and the undertones of ministerial discussions about monetary union, or about the relationship between enlarging the Community and deepening co-operation within it. My own realism in these matters almost led to my dismissal through a motion of censure in the European Parliament. But at least I was honest. After the 'First Europe' of a common market with rules binding on all, I wanted (and still want) a 'Second Europe' of habit-forming co-operation in as many areas of policy-making as appropriate. Some of this might well be *à la carte*, so that members of the Community can pick and choose whether they want to participate; in other respects non-members should be invited to participate. In this way, European realities would be created which provide the necessary material for building a constitution of a united Europe one day.

Perhaps this is too pragmatic; my colleague and much-respected mentor Altiero Spinelli certainly thought so. It may even be lacking in vision and emphasise unduly the co-operative aspect of Europe as against integration in the strict sense. If this is so, the reason is that my vision will forever be the Kantian project of a 'world civil society' with truly international institutions to guide and to sustain it. But none of this can detract from my commitment to pulling Europe closer together in areas of policy in which it is clearly the appropriate space. Today, they include not just a common market, but money and defence as well.

The German position is less clear. If I were asked for conclusive proof, I could probably not produce it, but my impression is that in an important sense Europe has remained a fair-weather concept for the majority of leading German politicians, and for many of their advisers as well. German professions of Europeanism are not insincere, but when something comes along that is regarded as more important, they are quickly forgotten; and such more important matters have come up in marginal as well as central policy areas. Germany likes Europe, but Europe does not have the priority and above all the reality in its political life which the Sunday sermons of its leaders would suggest. Chancellor Kohl has met President Mitterrand dozens of times, but these meetings have left him quite capable of announcing his 'ten points' for German unity in November 1989, two days after their last encounter, without even thinking of picking up the phone and telling his friend. The German government agrees to a process of European economic and monetary union, but moves without much thought about the implications forward to German monetary union first, though it is clear that the immediate need will have a significant effect on Community plans. German unity has many other European ramifications, some technical, some political; but when the key decisions were taken there was no sign of awareness as one would expect it in terms of the declared European commitment. Small wonder that Germany's European partners are bewildered and apprehensive! Even Germany's most reliable friend in France, the political scientist and commentator Alfred Grosser, wonders whether 'the united Germany might dissociate itself from the European Community and dominate it by its larger economic power'; though he dismisses the suspicion.

All this ties up with deeper concerns which are

rarely voiced, though present, in the minds of many Europeans as well as Americans and others. In some ways, Germany is seen as the Japan of Europe. This is not just a reference to balance-of-trade and balance-of-payments surpluses, but to a prevailing 'culture' (as some say for want of a better word) which is hard to penetrate. The corporatist ball of wax which includes government, big banks, key companies, trade unions, state-owned media and other recognised institutions has something to do with it. Why is it that in a decade of mergers and takeovers German business has remained relatively immune? People also sense a deeper resistance to things foreign, despite many outward signs to the contrary. In any case, Germany remains mysterious. If the mystery is combined with the shocks of unity, the apparent arrogance of leading political figures, and the openly voiced doubts of German intellectuals, the resulting mix is at best disagreeable and at worst highly inflammable.

But I must stop spreading doubts because it is not my intention to put you off either Germany or Europe. Speculation apart, I believe that your western border is one of the safest borders in Europe. Should Germany ever try to touch it, the whole of Europe would rise to your defence. Moreover, my bottom line says that the united Germany is not likely to be very different from the Federal Republic before it. This means among other things that the process of European co-operation and perhaps integration will advance further. Timetables will be upset every now and again, and the destination may in some sense remain unknown, but the next steps are fairly clear, and I want to trace them in so far as they are relevant for East Central Europe.

When Europe awoke from the gloom and doom of the 1970s, it defined as its goal what has come to be called 1992. The project is ambitious and important. Its thrust was, and is, to create by 31 December 1992 that common market which the Treaty of Rome foresaw long ago. However a common market means more in the 1990s than it did in the 1950s. At the time, the main barrier to be removed was that of tariffs; the 'four freedoms' which are now the objective barely mention this outdated obstacle to trade. Free movement of goods is impeded by many non-tariff barriers. Free movement of services and of capital requires major measures of liberalisation. Free movement of people may affect millions and will be tangible for all carriers of a burgundy-red European Community passport.

The Commission in Brussels decided that 279 legal instruments would have to be promulgated for 1992 to come about. This is normal politics, if ever it existed! No doubt some of the more important directives and regulations will founder. They are likely to involve the sacred cows of domestic politics, like zero VAT for children's clothes in Britain, and for books in France, or monopolistic suppliers of public services in Germany. But the movement towards opening borders among the twelve member states of the European Community seems unstoppable. What is more, if one adds up all the new legal instruments, the effect is more than the sum of 279. Normal politics gets close to the constitutional dimension if a large set of related signals all point in one direction. The Commission wants to use the momentum to go one or two steps further. Already, political co-operation has become an entrenched habit among the Twelve; ministers and officials know each other well enough to lift the phone when anything of relevance comes up and ring their colleagues in the Hague or in Rome or in Bonn. Now, monetary union is firmly on the agenda.

Monetary union is a grand and difficult project, more difficult perhaps than those convey who try to press it into the straitjacket of a *plan per étapes*, a plan in two or three stages. The problems are partly technical, though these can probably be overcome. They are partly political as well. Countries have to be ready to join in a monetary union which means, for example, that they must have institutions and policies in place which sustain a stable common currency. The commitment in principle to bring and keep inflation down to zero is one of the relevant policies, and it has to be the consensus of parties in all countries. Readiness to leave the responsibility for monetary stability to an independent central bank is an institutional prerequisite; for many it involves a break with long-standing traditions. France was not ready to take these steps when monetary union was launched for the first time in 1971, but today it is; the problem is Britain's reluctance to abandon the old Keynesian precept that $2\frac{1}{2}$ to 3 per cent inflation are not too bad, because 'nobody would notice', and to renounce the primacy of the Treasury over the Bank. Even if all these obstacles are overcome, there are the vagaries of the world market, and notably the currency markets, to be reckoned with. They can upset the best-laid plans, as they have done before.

Thus the road to monetary union is arduous, and I have not even mentioned the most complex issue which is, as usual, Germany. For one thing, GEMU, German monetary union, is bound to delay EMU, European monetary union. There is just not enough expert time to achieve both at once. More important, however, any European monetary system is bound to reflect the powerful position if not of Germany then of the deutschmark. The deutschmark may not quite play the role in EMU which the dollar played in the Bretton Woods system, but its movements will affect the others more than those of the French franc or even the pound sterling (assuming that Britain is a part of the process). It does not require German unity for Germany to be the strongest power in the European Community; indeed the process of unification may be so costly for Germany that for a while its claims to hegemony are weakened rather than strengthened. This may be a good moment to test Germany's preparedness to accept rules which are as binding on it as on others. Certainly, the momentum of European unification has a great deal to do with the German problem.

I believe that European monetary union will and should happen, though it will not come about either as quickly or as systematically as the Delors Plan, which foresees among other things a European Central Bank within the next three years, suggests. Monetary union is in a sense a part of the 1992 process. But the whole process is no longer the only or even the major issue. An Irish minister is said to have opened a conference on these matters with the words: 'Ladies and gentlemen, one thing is certain: 1992 will come.' Pause. 'The only question is, when?' The story is told as a joke, but it has a serious point. As I write this letter in 1990, I wonder if perhaps the European Community should say now: '1992 is here!' The objective of the great plan for revitalising Europe is achieved. We must now look forward to new horizons.

As we do so, the first issue is, who belongs and who does not. There are many outside Europe who fear, and a few within who hope, that the European Community of 1992 will turn into a well-provisioned fortress, protected by massive walls and a moat from those who do not belong. This need not happen. In fact, negotiations with the six remaining countries of EFTA are encouraging. It is true that the EFTA countries cannot have their cake and eat it; they cannot hope to enjoy the benefits of the Community without sharing the burdens, but above all, they cannot remain outside and yet be a part of the decision-making process. The idea of a European Economic Space (EES) which extends the economic advantages of the common market to EFTA but draws the line at political and institutional participation, is the beginning of an answer. Who knows? one day there may even be a European Economic Space Agency. I for one would hope that the EC will err on the side of generosity rather than meanness as it organises its relations with the developed democratic countries of Europe which for one reason or another do not want to be members of the Community.

Where does all this leave East Central Europe? The debate within the Community is heating up. There are those who argue, as one expert put it, 'that a further strengthening of the EC will make it more difficult for Eastern Europe to become more closely associated; or believe that, anyway, a looser structure in an enlarged but less concentrated EC would be more comfortable and indeed more realistic in an age in which national identities remain very powerful.' Prime Minister Thatcher inclines to this view, and German leaders must be tempted to adopt it. EC President Delors took the opposite line in his 1990 annual address to the European Parliament: 'The Twelve have no choice but to remain a focal point, a rock of stability for the rest of the continent.' A Europe on the road to integration is a 'lodestar' for the countries of Eastern Europe, and they will be as disappointed as anyone if the EC abandons its ambitions to become ever more close-knit, monetary union and all. 'We are duty-bound to help them' create conditions at home which one day make it possible but also attractive for them to become full members, and therefore we must not be deflected by apparent objectives of short-term relevance. Our aim is not 'Mr Gorbachev's dream of a "common European house",' but the 'slightly different vision of a

"European village" built around a solid house called the "European Community".' I agree with Jacques Delors.

Note that Delors did not use the language of European federalism! He even dissociated himself mildly from President Mitterrand's 'grand European confederation' which, he said, 'will not come into being until the Community achieves political union. It will be for each country to decide when the time comes.' No doubt each country will decide in its own time. I noticed that you regarded President Havel's idea of closer co-operation between Czechoslovakia, Poland and Hungary with a mixture of sympathy and scepticism. Emperor Franz Josef's rule may have been (in retrospect at least) the most benevolent regime which all of you had in this troubled century, but the dream of a new Habsburg Empire is little more than a nice conversation piece now. In terms of history and culture, the countries of East Central Europe are as different from each other as those of West Central Europe, and in terms of politics they are a long way from the threshold to a world of pooled sovereignty. We in the West reached that threshold a long time ago, probably in the 1950s. The war had left the old nation-states weary. France and Germany were beginning to explore a new, special relationship. While the return of the Saarland to Germany was based on a referendum in 1955 in which Europeanisation was decisively rejected, the process did not arouse great nationalist feelings; in effect the ease with which it was accomplished rather confirmed that nation-states had begun to matter less. The Marshall Plan helped bind the countries of Europe together; indeed for a long time, the United States behaved like a federator rather than a hegemonic power.

Economic developments contributed to the process. Once again the Saar, as well as Lorraine, the Liège basin and the Ruhr tell a story. For over a century the theory had been that if you possess iron ore, you had to get coal, and vice versa; now a European Coal and Steel Community was created. For many companies, national boundaries ceased to be relevant. Transnational companies – not always European – paved the way. If one likes the language, one could describe them as the great productive force which made the old, national relations of production seem hopelessly outdated. Pooling sovereignty was the only hope countries had to keep a degree of control over their affairs.

I am not unaware of the fact that some of the most thoughtful spokesmen of East Central Europe foresee similar developments for your part of the world. The notion of 'Benelux' has almost become a political 'Sweden', that is, an ideal which may not have as much to do with reality as its proponents think. Like you, I am a sceptic in this respect. As I look at the post-communist countries, I can see nation-states greatly in fashion. This is a good thing for independence and for the rule of law, as well as for seeking your own way forward into the open society. But it has its drawbacks, and you mentioned one of them, balkanisation. Who knows how many countries of

Europe there are going to be to the East and South-East of the borders of the European Community by the year 2000? And what are relations between them and their neighbours going to be like? Border incidents between the Baltic States and Greater Russia? Accusations of Polish interference in Lithuania as well as in the old Polish territories east of Brest-Litovsk? Continued indecision about the side on which the Moldavians' bread is buttered? Riotous demands for self-government in Transylvania? Quarrelling republics in Yugoslavia? The scenarios for trouble are numerous.

Behind this potential of fragmentation and friction lies one very serious issue. While we in Western Europe are concerned with pooling our sovereignty, you in Eastern Europe prefer to think about self-determination. This is easy to understand. Where would you be, were it not for the invocation of the principle of self-determination which is enshrined in all kinds of treaties and covenants, not least in the Helsinki Agreement? (It turned out to be one of two dynamic factors – the other being human rights – in that Agreement, for which otherwise neither you nor I have a great deal of time.) And yet self-determination has its problems. It was of course one of President Wilson's Fourteen Points of January 1918, though he was careful to say that 'in determining all such questions of sovereignty, the interests of the populations concerned must have equal weight with the equitable claims of the governments whose title is to be determined.' As he came to practical matters, however, he threw caution (and earlier ideas of a Central European Commonwealth) to the wind. 'The peoples of Austria-Hungary, whose place among the nations we wish to see safeguarded and assured, should be accorded the freest opportunity of autonomous development.' The notion of balkanisation goes back to the nineteenth century, but it acquired new virulence after 1919 and is once again highly relevant today.

The idea of national self-determination has its attractions for people who feel lost in the modern world. It appears to offer a sense of belonging and of meaning, embodied in powerful symbols like flags and anthems as well as passports and constitutions. People, some people at any rate, are prepared to die for the independence of their nation. It would be wrong to discount such a powerful force. Yet as a principle of international law, national self-determination is one of the more unfortunate inventions. It ascribes a right to peoples when rights should always be those of individuals. As a result, it invites usurpers to claim this right on behalf of peoples in whose name they speak while at the same time trampling on minorities, and sometimes on the civil rights of all. Who talks of those in Lithuania who do not want secession? Do their rights not matter? The Swiss may have had their own reasons when they rejected the decision by the overwhelming majority of the people of the Austrian province of Vorarlberg to join the Swiss Confederation in 1920, but the argument that they did not want the dissenting minority makes sense. If one allows the so-called right to self-determination to prevail over the basic rights of individual citizens, the result is likely to be a nation-state without liberty, and there is no shortage of examples.

The principle of self-determination also encourages homogeneity. Self-determining peoples will not tolerate a Nagorno-Karabakh in their midst. Once again, the result is the violent assertion of superior claims backed by majorities against defenceless minorities. It may be that there is some case for enabling historical units of people, even if they do not live on an island, to organise their own affairs if they so wish; but 'they' must never be allowed to violate the more elementary rights to the integrity of the person and to freedom of expression and of movement which are shared by all. Self-determination is at best a second-order right, far behind the civil, political and social rights of citizenship, and it is probably no right at all but merely a claim staked by populist leaders who may take their people to the open society but are just as likely to replace the serfdom of alien rule by that of indigenous tyranny.

Not in Poland! the advocates of Polish independence in freedom might say, and I hope they are right. Not in Czechoslovakia or in Hungary either, though we will no doubt hear Slovak and other minority voices to the contrary. In any case, I am well aware that this outburst against self-determination runs counter to all prevailing trends in the post-communist world. In his address to the European Parliament from which I have already quoted generously, Commission President Delors pointed out 'that Spain and Portugal spent seven years preparing for Community membership'. The economic reasons against immediate membership of any country in East Central Europe are overwhelming. It is hard enough to enter the home-grown valley of tears without adding the cost of joining a wider common market of free economies. But the factor which clinches the matter is the fundamental difference in orientation between countries which cherish their new-found national freedom, and others which have become wearily aware of the limitations of traditional notions of sovereignty. It has been said that while Western Europe is leaving the twentieth century for the twenty-first, Eastern Europe is leaving the twentieth century for the nineteenth. This may be an overstatement, but clearly we are not yet in tune all over Europe, and it will take some time before we are. What is more, we cannot really help you while you come to terms with sovereignty and self-determination in modern Europe, except by setting an example of how the joint exercise of sovereignty in certain areas of normal and even of constitutional politics adds to liberty and prosperity rather than detracting from it.

In the meantime, the idea of Europe's new architecture is emphatically not that the new democracies should remain outside and press their noses against the shop windows of progress. So far as membership is concerned, I have already mentioned the Council of Europe. Its statutes refer to the will of the people within its autonomous member-states, but the European Convention of Human Rights gives firm priority to the rights of individuals under the rule of law. You may wish to consider, along with the rest of us, the future of the OECD, which grew after all out of the Marshall Plan and has more experience of problems of economic development in Europe than anyone else. Beyond that, the European Community will, if it follows the lead of President Delors, undoubtedly try the almost unmanageable and pursue new forms of association with all non-members in Europe in parallel with the completion of the 1992 project, monetary union and a treaty with the remaining EFTA countries.

So far, this architecture of Europe must seem rather loose. It also does little, too little perhaps, to guard against the threats which your compatriots above all others perceive if to the East the Soviet empire crumbles, and to the West the already formidable power of Germany increases further. The image of the European village is fine so far as it goes, but there are many kinds of villages – some scattered, some huddled, some stretched along seemingly endless roads, some concentrated around the church or (as the more secular man, Jacques Delors, prefers) around the 'solid house called the "European Community"' – and all of them are difficult to police and to protect. Village feuds are among the most vicious fights between men, and women, and great wars have reduced villages to rubble without leaving as much as a ruin to remember where they were.

Policing within, like all law and order, depends in the last analysis on social control, that is, on neighbours caring without meddling all the time. This is hard enough to bring about; it has to do with civil society and building institutions; but those committed to the European construction are aware of the task. Protection without raises far more difficult issues. It brings in the Soviet Union, and the United States of America, of which little has been said so far. The Soviet Union does not look as if it can be a power which encourages and guarantees an order of Europe for some time to come. Its dominant concern is bound to be with its internal affairs, with holding together whatever is left of the Union, and with finding a way out of the mess which a half-hearted *perestroika* has added to a half-dismantled command system of administrative centralism. One cannot rule out circumstances in which these domestic problems may tempt leaders less responsible than President Gorbachev to seek temporary internal relief by external aggression, but one can rule out the Soviet Union as a power which impresses a notion of order on Europe without force.

Many have observed that as this is happening, the United States has embarked on one of its periodical retreats into its own shell. This is no doubt an exaggeration. Felix Rohatyn has stated persuasively, 'I do not believe that this is a correct analysis, but more and more, in Europe and in Japan, the US is seen as a marginal country.' Sometimes one is tempted to compare the United States with the friend who is standing behind a thick glass pane at an airport and watching events in the arrival hall. He sees his associates arrive and rush about; he can wave to them but cannot talk (except 'read my lips'); things happen over which the waiting friend has no control; he is there and yet not there, always visible but never involved. Again, this is less than the whole truth. Joseph Nye has taken on the growing gaggle of doomsters who wallow in America's sense of decline and pointed out that the United States may no longer be in a league by itself, but it is still clearly at the top of the world league of military, economic and political power as well as sheer attractiveness to millions of people. America is therefore 'bound to lead'.

Yet it is not leading as the revolution in Europe progresses. Perhaps we should not be too upset about the absence of the USA. At least no one will ever say that the revolution in Europe was a CIA conspiracy. Nor is there any evidence for arguing that the countries of East Central Europe have left the Soviet embrace in order to go to bed with the United States. More seriously, it is objectively difficult to see what the role of NATO is going to be, and how the Atlantic relationship fits into the European construction. Michael Howard has tried, and I agree with his objectives. The probability of 'a special military status for the nations of Central Europe' combined with the fact that 'there *is* a German problem' – 'It may be only a problem of perception, but it exists none the less' – means that an alliance without the US would be unacceptable. In any case, Howard concludes, 'if the price of reconstructing Europe is to be the disintegration of the Atlantic community, then we will have made a very bad bargain.' But what follows from such laudable objectives in practice?

I am not sure, and so far as I can see nobody has as yet made a convincing proposal. I would like to think that Britain has a special role to play in designing the security architecture of a future Europe. After all, Britain was well-prepared when the last crisis of this kind, if not quite of these proportions, occurred in 1954 after the French Parliament failed to ratify the treaty to set up a European Defence Community. Admittedly, the issue then was simpler than it is today. Germany's membership of NATO, and the British commitment to station an army on the Rhine (BAOR), created the additional guarantees needed at the time for Europe's security against a Soviet attack.

Today, it is difficult even to identify the problem. Who has to be defended against whom? The answers are bewildering and uncertain. The residual threat of Soviet Russia is not to be underrated; some would argue that it is more than residual, and that great powers have proved unpredictable before when they came under pressure. New threats could arise from within Europe. For decades now it has been accepted wisdom that the age of wars between European countries is over. This is probably still true. But as one watches the emergence not only of new nations but of old national emotions, one must be allowed to wonder a little. Certainly security within the wider Europe from Brest, or rather from Galway in western

Ireland, to Brest, if not to Vilnius and Riga, needs guarantees which do not exist today. Then there are the many sources of instability all over the world. Not all involve Europe but some do, partly because of their proximity and partly because they invoke historical relationships. A less structured world is also a more precarious world, and it is well to be prepared for trouble.

How? For the moment, confusion rules absolute, all the way to the suggestion that a united Germany should belong simultaneously to NATO and the Warsaw Pact. This will clearly not happen. As an effective military alliance, the Warsaw Pact has all but disappeared, but NATO too is going through an agonising reappraisal. If I were to speculate for a moment, I would expect three developments in the years to come. One would be an arrangement between the nuclear superpowers which satisfies the security concerns of the Soviet Union while reducing the level of nuclear as well as conventional armament. A second development would be designed to link the countries of Europe in a kind of CETO, a Central European Treaty Organisation. Since it would extend from Ireland to Poland and perhaps beyond, its military content would be less impressive than its political intent. The third development would have to be Atlantic. A redefined relationship between the United States and Europe would have to be based on NATO and backed up by military guarantees, though their nature and extent need much thought. History and geography alike give Britain a central position in such deliber-

145

ations, although Germany is bound to be their central concern.

These ideas are vague and leave more questions open than they answer. One must hope that we have the time to work them out without unpleasant surprises. It may help that we have already entered a new stage in the construction of Europe which is one of negotiation. Numbers have been bandied about: 2 (Germanies) plus 4 ('victor' powers) plus 8 (German neighbours other than France), plus 12 (countries in the European Community), then 16 (NATO members) and 35 (participant countries in the CSCE). If all this, or even some of it, happens, we will know that history has slowed down again. I suppose we are all a bit out of breath after the hectic rush of 1989, and the rougher ride of 1990, so that we can do with a more measured pace. Changing gear, as I said before, has its own risks; I hope we keep our nerve as it happens. However, one niggling thought which accompanies this process must be brought to the open. The revolution in Europe has been in the headlines for quite a long time. It has actually put a welcome strain on people's attention span which has sadly been much reduced by the apparent need for tabloids and television to go for the immediate and the sensational. But East Central Europe is not likely to stay in the headlines forever. By the time the slow-moving machine of publishing has churned out the library of books on the subject which are now being written, the products may not only be out of date but out of most people's minds because other subjects have rushed to prominence.

They might even be international subjects. The Middle East has retreated from public attention while everyone stared at Warsaw and Prague and Berlin, but it is no less explosive for that. China after Tiananmen Square will not be stable again until it accommodates pressures for change rather than suppressing them brutally. We all have to prepare for a time when the release of 500 million dollars' worth of aid takes governments and parliaments as long as it normally does, which could be years or even an eternity, rather than a few days under the influence of a visit by your Prime Minister or the President of Czechoslovakia. This if nothing else is the reason why ultimately you will have to rely on your own resources. By that I do not necessarily, and certainly not only mean your material resources. Generous assistance from the rest of Europe and also from the United States and Japan should cushion the painful journey through the valley of tears. But I do mean resources of good sense and of courage, human resources on the part of the lawyers, the politicians and above all the citizens.

Somehow I mind the imminent prospect of normality. The reason is not just my penchant for constitutional politics, but also the invigorating quality of a revolution which opens up prospects of liberty. Examples of the victory of men of great integrity who demonstrate the courage of their convictions make all of us feel that from time to time good can prevail over evil in this world. Normality is not very inspiring in this respect as in others. But then reasoned thought gets the better of my passions. Perhaps a deeper passion directs it away from the immediate. Many people all over the world have watched the spectacle of the revolution in Europe with some resentment. They feel left out. Unlike Americans they are not sympathetic onlookers who see their friends arrive and indeed come home, but forgotten victims of their own predicaments of terror, starvation and disease. Who now talks about Ethiopia? About Burma?

The peoples of East Central Europe have been living a dreadful but also a sheltered life behind the Iron Curtain. For them the world scene was a faraway battleground of great powers and international organisations, a continuation of the Cold War by political means. The reunifications resulting from the revolution of 1989 have changed this too. All European nations are now a part of a world in which responsibility does not end at one's own front door. I am not suggesting that the record of the European Community (for example) is unblemished in this respect. The Kennedy Round and the agreements of Yaounde and Lome with developing countries notwithstanding, we have undoubtedly violated international rules at times, and have failed to do enough for those in need. But this is no excuse for the old Europe, or the new one which is now emerging, to ignore the rest of the world.

I have been rather harsh with President Gorbachev and his notion of a common European house. However, careful observers have noticed that he himself has long begun to play down the notion in favour of an emphasis on global issues which unite mankind rather than dividing it into blocs. Lasting peace is one such issue, and we must hope that the speed of progress with respect to disarmament and arms control arrangements which is now in the cards is not slowed down by the onset of normality. Development is another world issue, and your own experience should remind all that this cannot just mean economic improvement but has to be linked to recognised human rights and chances of participation for citizens. The human habitat on this planet has climbed to the top of the agenda of governments, international organisations and many individuals. The state of the environment in Eastern Europe tells a sorry tale about the consequences of neglecting this issue. It is also one which requires a critical balance of decisive international action and the commitment to preserve elementary freedoms. The benevolent dictatorship of ecologist-kings would be no better than any other dictatorship, and we must beware.

The point of these reminders is simple. Living in a solid house is a pleasing prospect. A well-policed village which is sure of its defences gives its inhabitants a sense of security and the chance to get on with their business. But the village is a part of a much larger landscape of human settlements. What happens in one of them affects what happens in all the others. In particular, those in the solid house have an effect on everyone else whatever they do or do not do. This is even more clearly the case for those in the skyscraper across the waters. In the end we will not be safe or free unless people in all the villages and towns of the world are citizens.

Dear Mr J., it is time to draw this long epistle to a close. Apart from all other reasons, one should always finish when one is inclined to become lyrical. I have taken the opportunity of your questions to say more about some of them than you may have bargained for. Let me assure you that this is not for want of trying to be concise and clear. The simple fact is that your questions, and the entire process of the revolution in Europe, stir the mind and the heart of a liberal deeply.

Nor is the intention of this letter purely theoretical. My main point is simple. The choice with which we are faced in organising our affairs is that between systems of whatever description and the open society. There is no third way, and I am delighted that you have chosen the road to freedom. On this road there is space for many speeds and methods of travel, and also for detours and byways, though rarely for short cuts. Within the constitution of liberty a hundred ways lead forward, and all of them are likely to mix elements of economic, political and social reform in ways which offend the purist. The key to progress is therefore not a complete alternative conception, a detailed master plan of freedom. Such plans are contradictions in terms and more likely to lead back to the closed society. The key to progress is strategic change. It is to identify a small number of seemingly minor decisions which are likely to have major long-term effects and ramifications. Strategic changes are measures which have high leverage and often touch the margin of what is acceptable and practicable in given conditions, but they are not about systems and their changes.

Karl Popper, to whose thinking I owe more than to any other author, has sung the praises of 'piecemeal *versus* Utopian engineering'. I know what he means though for once I do not care for his language. Even apart from the unfortunate connotations of social engineering, 'piecemeal' is not quite enough when one is faced with a constitutional challenge. Popper leaves the door open to 'the possibility that a series of piecemeal reforms might be inspired by one general tendency'. Certainly it helps to have an image of the future. But the critical question is how one gets from here to there, and the answer must be by taking the all-important first steps in the right direction. Ludwig Erhard's reforms can hardly be called piecemeal, nor can those of Leszek Balcerowicz, or indeed Vaclav Havel's decisions to expropriate party property and suspend teachers of Marxism-Leninism.

In the nature of the case, there is no general rule for identifying appropriate strategic decisions. The situation differs from place to place and from time to time, and I am impatient with those who peddle patent medicines, be they immediate convertibility of the currency or the single transferable vote in elections. My hunch is that in Poland, the initial strategic changes have in fact been made, and the task is to stick with them and see them through, while perhaps adding a bit of social policy to the economic reforms.

In East Germany, the strategic needs were easily identified; monetary and political union with the Federal Republic are obvious goals. It may well be that in Czechoslovakia the political and constitutional changes which the first free government initiated have set the right course, though much remains to be done on the economic side. Others, including Hungary, find themselves in a more difficult position, if only because the collapse of the centre has gone further. Much depends in such a situation on using the remaining powers of government to good purpose. It is possible that this leads to giving primacy to decisions in the monetary field, coupled of course with attempts to reconstruct at least a rudimentary machinery of government.

Can we help? Indeed, should we help? Much depends on what East Central Europeans and their governments want. In some cases, there is a clear need for emergency aid. The Group of 24, under the leadership of the European Community, has taken the need on board ever since the World Economic Summit in Strasburg gave it the task. I hope the European Bank for Recovery and Development will not get bogged down in a quagmire of rivalries and bureaucratic difficulties. Too many Marshall Plans have been demanded by over-eager committees and individuals in recent years. They forget many facts, including the sheer magnitude of the post-war operation itself, when the United States made available no less than 2 per cent of its GDP for five years to help Europe recover. Moreover, the Marshall Plan had its relative failures as well as spectacular successes. Still, if the rest of Europe were prepared to make available 2 per cent of our GDP for five years running to help the transitions of post-communist countries, I for one would be happy to support the parties and governments which promote the project.

Then there is the great task of civil society. It is the most important of all, and of course the one which requires the greatest efforts in the countries concerned. We may be able to convey some know-how in a number of fields. Thinking back to post-war Germany I remember with gratitude the availability of books and journals, of exchange schemes for travel, even of conferences and symposia; though I hear that you begin to feel swamped by invitations and an invasion of Western visitors. Yet reunifying language is not enough if this remains an unused opportunity rather than a challenge to practise the common language, and to do so often and everywhere. Too much contact and discussion is better than too little. A great deal remains to be done, most of it by you, your compatriots and those elsewhere in the new democracies of Europe who are seeking the road to freedom.

It is hard to do better than Edmund Burke in ending this letter, for I too 'have told you candidly of my sentiments'. But perhaps Burke was a little too pessimistic, adding, 'I think they are not likely to alter yours.' I on the contrary hope that you will reconsider some of your less persuasive ambitions, like 'Sweden', the 'third way' and 'Central Europe'. 'I have little to recommend my opinions but long observation and much impartiality ... They come from one, almost the whole of whose public exertion has been a struggle for the liberty of others.' I also like the way Edmund Burke winds up his epistle by describing himself as one who 'when the equipoise of the vessel in which he sails may be endangered by over-loading it upon one side, is desirous of carrying the small weight of his reasons to that which may preserve its equipoise'. Is there a more measured way of describing a counter-cyclical view of things? Liberty above all is what I believe in. The goal may be obvious but the path to it has many pitfalls. We can help master some of them, but for the most part your own energy and sense of purpose are called for. The rest is luck. I keep my fingers crossed and hope for the best. This I do with all my heart.

Very sincerely yours,

R.D.

Oxford, April 1990

About the Author

SIR RALF DAHRENDORF was born in Hamburg in 1929. He read Philosophy and Classics in Hamburg and Sociology in London before embarking on an academic career as a sociologist. In 1967 he went into politics in his native Germany, where he became a Member of Parliament and a government minister before he went to Brussels in 1970 as an EC Commissioner. In 1974 he came to Britain, first as Director of the London School of Economics (1974–84) and since 1987 as Warden of St Anthony's College, Oxford. His books include *Class and Class Conflict in Industrial Society* (1959), *Society and Democracy in Germany* (1967), *On Britain* (1982) and *The Modern Social Conflict* (1989).

Also available in bookshops now:-

Forthcoming Chatto Counter*Blasts*

Forthcoming **Counter*Blasts*** (and Specials) include Shirley Hazzard on Waldheim and the United Nations, Brenda Maddox on the Pope and birth control, and Stephen Fry on education.

If you want to join in the debate, and if you want to know more about Counter*Blasts*, the writers and the issues, then write to:

Random Century Group, Freepost 5066, Dept MH, London SW1V 2YY